California Real Estate Salesperson Practice Exams for 2014

by

Jim Bainbridge, J.D.

Member of the California State Bar

and

California Real Estate Broker

City Breeze Publishing
P.O. Box 12650
Marina del Rey, CA 90295

DISCLAIMER and LIMIT of LIABILITY

THIS WORK IS PROVIDED "AS IS." NEITHER THE AUTHOR NOR THE PUBLISHER MAKE ANY WARRANTY OR GUARANTEE AS TO THE ACCURACY OR COMPLETENESS OF THIS WORK, OR TO RESULTS TO BE OBTAINED FROM THIS WORK, AND EXPRESSLY DISCLAIM ANY EXPRESS OR IMPLIED WARRANTY, INCLUDING BUT NOT LIMITED TO IMPLIED WARRANTIES OF MARKETABILITY OR FITNESS FOR A PARTICULAR PURPOSE.

Though the author and publisher have taken care in the writing and publishing of this work, they make no express or implied warranty of any kind, assume no responsibility for errors or omissions, and assume no liability for incidental or consequential damages arising out of, or in connection with, the use of the information contained in this work. This limitation of liability shall apply to any claim or cause of action, regardless of whether such claim or cause of action arises in contract, tort, or otherwise.

This work is provided for informational purposes only. It is not legal, accounting, or other professional advice, and it does not establish an attorney-client relationship with any person.

Table of Contents

Introduction

Thank you for purchasing *CALIFORNIA REAL ESTATE SALESPERSON PRACTICE EXAMS for 2014*. This book is intended to help you prepare for, and pass, the California real estate salesperson exam. This book contains:

- tips on preparing for and taking the exam;

- three 150-multiple-choice-question practice salesperson exams, with detailed answers given for all of the questions;

- a comprehensive glossary of over 600 key real estate terms; and

- a review of the math relevant to real estate practice that you are expected to know for the exam.

Of course, this book is no substitute for study of the California real estate pre-licensing courses that are required by the Bureau of Real Estate (the CalBRE). Before you take these practice exams, you should have a thorough knowledge of these required pre-licensing courses. If you do not, you may become discouraged by your scores on these practice exams — and confidence, in addition to study and practice, will serve you well on your quest to pass the salesperson exam and to become a California real estate licensee.

A textbook that you may find to be a valuable up-to-date review of all of these pre-licensing courses is *California Real Estate Principles and License Preparation, 2nd Edition*, by Jim Bainbridge, who is a graduate of Harvard Law School, a member of the California Bar, and a licensed California real estate broker.

Tips for Preparing for and Taking the Exam:

- Each of the following practice California salesperson exams consists (as do the official CalBRE salesperson exams) of 150 multiple-choice questions. You should give yourself 3 hours and 15 minutes to complete each exam, which should be completed in one sitting.

- When you check your answers to the exams, pay careful attention not only to the correct answer (a, b, c, or d), but also to the explanation of the answer to be sure that you answered the question correctly (if you did) for the right reason.

- You are graded on the number of correct answers you give. You are not penalized for giving incorrect answers. Therefore, it is important to answer all of the questions, even if you are not sure of the correct answer. Often, of the four possible answers given, at least two answers are clearly wrong. Of the remaining two, both might appear correct, in which case you should choose the answer that you feel is the better one. If you cannot decide which one is the better, take your best guess — you'll probably have about a 50-50 chance of being correct; and remember, you only need to score 70% to pass, so good guessing can make all the difference between passing and failing an exam.

- Take the time to read each question carefully. It is altogether too easy to interpret a question in a way that you expect the question to read, rather than as it is actually stated. This is especially true for questions that are stated in the negative ("it is not true that..." or "which of the following is false"). Other keywords that can significantly alter the meaning of a question are "except," "but," "if," "always," and "normally."

- Do not rush to choose an answer just because you are relatively certain that it is true. This is because there may be two or more answers given that correctly answer the question, in which case such answers as "both a and b" or "all of the above" may be the best, and correct, answer.

- If math is your most problematic and anxiety producing area, consider saving the math questions to the end and coming back to them when you have completed the rest of the exam. This will prevent you from becoming frustrated and discouraged through most of the exam and will likely give you more time to figure out the correct answers to the math questions.

- You should try to estimate the correct answer to math questions before you begin your calculations. If you find that your estimate is far different from the result of your calculation, carefully go back and check your calculation. Also, be aware that the possible answers presented for math questions usually contain answers that examinees can arrive at by making some common error, such as by calculating based on the number of years rather than on the number of months. Therefore, just because the result of your calculation exactly matches one of the possible answers does not mean that your result is correct.

- Because the extensive glossary included in the next section of this book includes terms often found on the real estate exams, it is recommended that you review these important key real estate terms at least once each week prior to taking the official CalBRE exam.

- Finally, if you complete the exam early, as many examinees do, take the remaining time to read over as many of the questions as you can to be sure that you did not make the all-too-common mistake of misreading certain questions the first time around. As you take the following practice exams, you will probably find that you make numerous "foolish" errors — errors that resulted not from your lack of knowledge, but from your failure to carefully read certain questions that can at times appear to be a bit tricky. Don't let such "foolish" errors spoil the result of your actual exam.

Good luck! And may you have a long and rewarding career as a California real estate licensee.

Definitions of Key Real Estate Terms

1031 exchange — under Internal Revenue Code section 1031, a tax-deferred exchange of "like kind" properties.

1031 exchange boot — cash and/or unlike property received in a 1031 exchange.

1099-S Reporting — a report to be submitted on IRS Form 1099-S by escrow agents to report the sale of real estate, giving the seller's name, Social Security number, and the gross sale proceeds.

30/360 day count convention — a convention for calculating interest or allocating expenses in which each month is considered to have 30 days, and each year is considered to have 360 days.

acknowledgment — a written declaration signed by a person before a duly authorized officer, usually a notary public, acknowledging that the signing is voluntary.

acknowledgment of satisfaction — a written declaration signed by a person before a duly authorized officer, usually a notary public, acknowledging that a lien has been paid off in full and that the signing is voluntary.

abandonment — failure to occupy or use property that may result in the extinguishment of a right or interest in the property.

abatement — a legal action to remove a nuisance.

abstract of judgment — a summary of the essential provisions of a court monetary judgment that can be recorded in the county recorder's office of the county or counties in which the judgment debtor owns property to create a judgment lien against such properties.

acceleration clause — a clause in either a promissory note, a security instrument, or both that states that upon default the lender has the option of declaring the entire balance of outstanding principal and interest due and payable immediately.

acceptance — consent (by an offeree) to an offer made (by an offeror) to enter into and be bound by a contract.

accession — the acquisition of additional property by the natural processes of accretion, reliction, or avulsion, or by the human processes of the addition of fixtures or improvements made in error.

accretion — a natural process by which the owner of riparian or littoral property acquires additional land by the gradual accumulation of soil through the action of water.

accrued depreciation — depreciation that has happened prior to the date of valuation.

acknowledgment — a written declaration signed by a person before a duly authorized officer, usually a notary public, acknowledging that the signing is voluntary.

acknowledgment of satisfaction — a written declaration signed by a person before a duly authorized officer, usually a notary public, acknowledging that a lien has been paid off in full and that the signing is voluntary.

active investor — an investor who actively contributes to the management of the business invested in.

actual agency — an agency in which the agent is employed by the principal, either by express agreement, ratification, or implication.

ad valorem — a Latin phrase meaning "according to value." The term is usually used regarding property taxation.

adjustable-rate mortgage (ARM) — a mortgage under which interest rates applicable to the loan vary over the term of the loan.

adjusted cost basis — the dollar amount assigned to a property after additions of improvements and deductions for depreciation and losses are made to the property's acquisition cost.

adjustment period — the time intervals in an adjustable-rate mortgage during which interest rates are not adjusted.

administrator — a person appointed by a probate court to conduct the affairs and distribute the assets of a decedent's estate when there was no executor named in the will or there was no will.

advance fee — a fee charged in advance of services rendered.

adverse possession — the process by which unauthorized possession and use of another's property can ripen into ownership of that other's property without compensation.

after-acquired interests — all interests in a property acquired subsequent to a transfer of the property.

age-life method — *see*, straight-line method.

agency — the representation of a principal by an agent.

agent — a person who represents another.

alienation clause — a due-on-sale clause

alluvium — addition to land acquired by the gradual accumulation of soil through the action of water.

ALTA policy — an extended title insurance policy developed by the American Land Title Association.

ambulatory instrument — a document that can be changed or revoked, such as a will.

amended public report — a report that a subdivider must apply for if, after the issuance of a final public report, new conditions arise that affect the value of the subdivision parcels.

Americans with Disabilities Act — a federal act that prohibits discrimination against persons with disabilities, where "disability" is defined as "a physical or mental impairment that substantially limits a major life activity."

amortization — in general, the process of decreasing or recovering an amount over a period of time; as applied to real estate loans, the process of reducing the loan principal over the life of the loan.

anchor bolt — a bolt inserted into concrete that secures structural members to the foundation.

annual percentage rate (APR) — expresses the effective annual rate of the cost of borrowing, which includes all finance charges, such as interest, prepaid finance charges, prepaid interest, and service fees.

appraisal — an estimate of the value of property resulting from an analysis and evaluation made by an appraiser of facts and data regarding the property.

appreciation — an increase in value due to any cause.

appropriation, right of — the legal right to take possession of and use for beneficial purposes water from streams or other bodies of water.

appurtenance — an object, right or interest that is incidental to the land and goes with or pertains to the land.

assignment — a transfer of a tenant's entire interest in the tenant's leased premises.

associate broker — a person with a real estate brokers license who is employed as a salesperson by another broker.

assumption — an adoption of an obligation that primarily rests upon another person, such as when a purchaser agrees to be primarily liable on a loan taken out by the seller.

attachment lien — a prejudgment lien on property, obtained to ensure the availability of funds to pay a judgment if the plaintiff prevails.

attorney in fact — a holder of a power of attorney.

automatic homestead —a homestead exemption that applies automatically to a homeowner's principal residence and that provides limited protection for the homeowner's equity in that residence against a judgment lien foreclosure.

avulsion — a process that occurs when a river or stream suddenly carries away a part of a bank and deposits it downstream, either on the same or opposite bank.

back-end ratio — the ratio of total monthly expenses, including housing expenses and long-term monthly debt payments, to monthly gross income.

balloon payment — a payment, usually the final payment, of an installment loan that is significantly greater than prior payments — "significantly greater" generally being considered as being more than twice the lowest installment payment paid over the loan term.

bankruptcy — a legal process conducted in a United States Bankruptcy court, in which a person declares his or her inability to pay debts.

base lines — in the Sections and Township method of land description, California has three sets of base lines, which are east-west lines, and meridians, which are north-south lines.

beam — a horizontal member of a building attached to framing, rafters, etc., that transversely supports a load.

bearing wall — a wall that supports structures (such as the roof or upper floors) above it. In condominiums, non-bearing walls are owned by the individual condominium owners, whereas bearing walls usually are property owned in common.

beneficiary — (1) the lender under a deed of trust, (2) one entitled to receive property under a will, (3) one for whom a trust is created.

bequeath — to transfer personal property by a will.

bequest — a gift of personal property by will.

bilateral contract — a contract in which a promise given by one party is exchanged for a promise given by the other party.

bill of sale — a written document given by a seller to a purchaser of personal property.

blanket mortgage — a mortgage used to finance two or more parcels of real estate.

blight — as used in real estate, the decline of a property or neighborhood as a result of adverse land use, destructive economic forces, failure to maintain the quality of older structures, failure to maintain foreclosed homes, etc.

11

blind ad — an advertisement that does not disclose the identity of the agent submitting the advertisement for publication.

blockbusting — the illegal practice of representing that prices will decline, or crime increase, or other negative effects will occur because of the entrance of minorities into particular areas.

board foot — a unit of measure of the volume of lumber, equivalent to the volume of lumber of 1 square foot and 1 inch thick; 144 cubic inches.

bona fide — in good faith; authentic; sincere; without intent to deceive.

book depreciation — a mathematical calculation used by tax authorities and accountants to determine a depreciation deduction from gross income.

book sale — a "sale" for accounting purposes regarding tax-delinquent property; this "sale" does not entail an actual transfer property.

bridge loan — a short-term loan (often referred to as a swing loan) that is used by a borrower until permanent financing becomes available.

broker — a person who, for a compensation or an expectation of compensation, represents another in the transfer of an interest in real property. A real estate broker must pass the CalBRE's brokers exam and be licensed as a real estate broker.

BTU (British Thermal Unit) — A measure of heating (or cooling) capacity equivalent to the amount of heat required to raise the temperature of 1 pound of water 1° Fahrenheit (from 39°F to 40°F).

bulk sale — a sale, not in the ordinary course of the seller's business, of more than half of the value of the seller's inventory as of the date of the bulk sale agreement.

bundle of rights — rights the law attributes to ownership of property.

business opportunity — involves the sale or lease of the assets of an existing business enterprise or opportunity, including the goodwill of the business or opportunity, enabling the purchaser or lessee to begin a business.

buyer's agent — a real estate broker appointed by a buyer to find property for the buyer.

California Association of Realtors® — the state organization of the National Association of Realtors®.

California Coastal Zone Conservation Act — a California state law that is intended to promote the preservation and protection of California's diverse coastal zone.

California Environmental Quality Act (CEQA) — a California state law that requires state and local agencies to consider and respond to the environmental effects of private and public development projects.

California Housing Finance Agency (CalHFA) — a California state agency that makes low-interest loans to "first-time homebuyers" from funds derived from the sale of tax-exempt bonds.

California Withholding Law — a California law that, with certain exceptions, requires the buyer of California real estate to withhold 3⅓% of the gross sales price from any individual seller.

CalVet loan — a loan made by the Farm and Home Loan Division of the DVA to eligible military veterans for the purchase of a home or farm in California.

capital asset — permanent, non-inventory assets held for personal or investment purposes, such as householders' homes, household furnishings, stocks, bonds, land, buildings, and machinery.

capital gain — the amount by which the net sale proceeds from the sale of a capital asset exceeds the adjusted cost value of the asset.

capitalization approach — *see*, income approach

capitalization rate — the annual net income of a property divided by the initial investment in, or value of, the property; the rate that an appraiser estimates is the yield rate expected by investors from comparable properties in current market conditions.

capture, law of — the legal right of a landowner to all of the gas, oil, and steam produced from wells drilled directly underneath on his or her property, even if the gas, oil, or steam migrates from below a neighbor's property.

carbon monoxide (CO) detector — a CO detector/alarm or a CO alarm combined with a smoke detector. As of January 1, 2013, CO detectors must be installed in all California dwelling units that contain a fossil fuel burning heater or appliance, a fireplace, or that have an attached garage.

Carbon Monoxide Poisoning Prevention Act — a California law that requires the installation of carbon monoxide alarms in most residential units.

carryover —under an adjustable-rate loan, an increase in the interest rate not imposed because of an interest-rate cap that is carried over to later rate adjustments.

Cartwright Act — the California legislative act that is the basis for California's antitrust laws.

caulking — a putty-like material used to seal cracks and joints to make tight against leakage of air or water, as in making windows watertight.

CC&Rs — an abbreviation of "covenants, conditions, and restrictions" — often used to refer to restrictions recorded by a developer on an entire subdivision.

certificate of clearance — a certificate issued by the Board of Equalization to the buyer of a business that states that no taxes, interest, or penalties are due from the seller or from any previous owner of the business.

certificate of discharge — a written instrument used to release a lien created by a mortgage.

Certificate of Eligibility — a certificate issued by the VA, certifying that the applicant is eligible for a VA-guaranteed loan of a certain amount.

Certificate of Reasonable Value (CRV) — a certificate issued by a VA-approved appraiser that certifies, pursuant to VA guidelines, the reasonable value of a property that is to be used as security for a VA-guaranteed loan.

chain of title — a complete chronological history of all of the documents affecting title to the property.

chattel real — personal property that contains some interest in real property, the most common example being a lease.

Civil Rights Act of 1866 — a federal law enacted during Reconstruction that stated that people of any race may enjoy the right to enforce contracts, to sue, be parties, and give evidence, to inherit, purchase, lease, sell, hold, and convey real and personal property, and to full and equal benefit of all laws.

Civil Rights Act of 1968 — a federal law (often referred to as the Fair Housing Act) that prohibited discrimination in housing based on race, creed, or national origin. An amendment to this Act in 1974 added prohibition against discrimination based on gender, and an amendment in 1988 added prohibition against discrimination based on a person's disabilities or familial status.

client — an agent's principal

closing — in reference to an escrow, a process leading up to, and concluding with, a buyer's receiving the deed to the property and the seller's receiving the purchase money.

CLTA policy — a standard title insurance policy developed by the California Land Title Association.

collar beam — a beam connecting pairs of opposite rafters well above the attic floor.

column — a circular or rectangular vertical structural member that supports the weight of the structure above it.

commercial acre — the buildable part of an acre that remains after subtracting land needed for streets, sidewalks, and curbs.

commingling — regarding trust fund accounts, the act of improperly segregating the funds belonging to the agent from the funds received and held on behalf of another; the mixing of separate and community property.

commission — an agent's compensation for performance of his or her duties as an agent; in real estate, it is usually a percent of the selling price of the property or, in the case of leases, of rentals.

common interest development (CID) — a subdivision in which purchasers own or lease a separate lot, unit, or interest, and have an undivided interest or membership in a portion of the common area of the subdivision.

community apartment project — a development in which an undivided interest in the land is coupled with the right of exclusive occupancy of an apartment located thereon.

community property — property owned jointly by a married couple or by registered domestic partners, as distinguished from separate property. As a general rule, property acquired by a spouse or registered domestic partner through his/her skills or personal efforts is community property.

community property with right of survivorship — property that is community property and that has a right of survivorship. Upon the death of a spouse or registered domestic partner, community property with right of survivorship passes to the surviving spouse or domestic partner without probate.

Community Redevelopment Law — a California state law that provides local governments with the authority to correct blighted conditions in areas within their jurisdictions.

comparable property — a property similar to the subject property being appraised that recently sold at arm's length, where neither the buyer nor the seller was acting under significant financial pressure.

compound interest — the type of interest that is generated when accumulated interest is reinvested to generate interest earnings from previous interest earnings.

concealment — the act of preventing disclosure of something.

condition subsequent — a condition written into the deed of a fee estate that, if violated, may "defeat" the estate and lead to its loss and reversion to the grantor.

conditional use — a zoning exception for special uses such as churches, schools, and hospitals that wish to locate to areas zoned exclusively for residential use.

condominium — a residential unit owned in severalty, the boundaries of which are usually walls, floors, and ceilings, and an undivided interest in portions of the real property, such as halls, elevators, and recreational facilities.

conduit — a (usually) metal pipe in which electrical wiring is installed.

conflict of interest — a situation in which an individual or organization is involved in several *potentially* competing interests, creating a risk that one interest *might* unduly influence another interest.

conforming loan — a loan in conformance with FHFA guidelines.

consideration — anything of value given or promised, such as money, property, services, or a forbearance, to induce another to enter into a contract.

conspiracy — in antitrust law, occurs when two or more persons agree to act and the agreed-upon action has the effect of restraining trade.

construction mortgage — a security instrument used to secure a short-term loan to finance improvements to a property.

constructive eviction — a breach by the landlord of the covenant of habitability or quiet enjoyment.

constructive notice — (1) notice provided by public records; (2) notice of information provided by law to a person who, by exercising reasonable diligence, could have discovered the information.

Constructors' State License Law — a California state law that, with certain exceptions, requires that every building contractor must be licensed by the Contractors' State License Board.

contingency — an event that may, but is not certain to, happen, the occurrence upon which the happening of another event is dependent.

conventional loan — a mortgage loan that is not FHA insured or VA guaranteed.

conversion — the unauthorized misappropriation and use of another's funds or other property.

cooperating broker — a broker who attempts to find a buyer for a property listed by another broker.

co-ownership — joint ownership

cost approach — an appraisal approach that obtains the market value of the subject property by adding the value of the land (unimproved) of the subject property to the depreciated value of the cost (if currently purchased new) of the improvements on subject property.

cost recovery — the recoupment of the purchase price of a property through book depreciation; the tax concept of depreciation.

Costa-Hawkins Rental Housing Act — a state law that places restrictions on local rent control laws.

cost-to-cure method — a method of calculating depreciation by estimating the cost of curing the curable depreciation and adding it to the value of the incurable depreciation.

counteroffer — a new offer by an offeree that acts as a rejection of an offer by an offeror.

coupled with an interest — an aspect of an agency that refers to the agent's having a financial interest in the subject of the agency.

covenant — a contractual promise to do or not do certain acts, the remedy for breach thereof being either monetary damages or injunctive relief, not forfeiture.

crawlspace — the space between the ground and the first floor that permits access beneath the building.

credit bid — a bid at a foreclosure sale made by the beneficiary up to the amount owed to the beneficiary.

credits — in reference to an escrow account, items payable to a party. This definition of a debit does not conform to its use in double-entry bookkeeping or accounting.

curable depreciation — depreciation that results from physical deterioration or functional obsolescence that can be repaired or replaced at a cost that is less than or equal to the value added to the property.

debits — in reference to an escrow account, items payable by a party. This definition of a debit does not conform to its use in double-entry bookkeeping or accounting.

declared homestead — the dwelling described in a homestead declaration.

deed — a document that when signed by the grantor and legally delivered to the grantee conveys title to real property.

deed in lieu of foreclosure — a method of avoiding foreclosure by conveying to a lender title to a property lieu of the lender's foreclosing on the property.

defeasance clause — a provision in a loan that states that when the loan debt has been fully paid, the lender must release the property from the lien so that legal title free from the lien will be owned by the borrower.

defendant — the one against whom a lawsuit is brought.

deferred maintenance — any type of depreciation that has not been corrected by diligent maintenance.

deficiency judgment — a judgment given to a lender in an amount equal to the balance of the loan minus the net proceeds the lender receives after a judicial foreclosure.

demand — the level of desire for a product.

deposit receipt — a written document indicating that a good-faith deposit has been received as part of an offer to purchase real property; also called a purchase and sale agreement.

depreciation — the loss in value due to any cause.

depreciation deduction — an annual tax allowance for the depreciation of property.

devise — (1) (noun) a gift of real property by will; (2) (verb) to transfer real property by a will.

devisee — a recipient of real property through a will.

disabled veteran's exemption — and exemption that can reduce the tax liability of a qualified veteran's principal place of residence.

discounted rate — a rate (also called a teaser rate) on an adjustable-rate mortgage that is less than the fully indexed rate.

discount points — a form of prepaid interest on a mortgage, or a fee paid to a lender to cover cost the making of a loan. The fee for one discount point is equal to 1% of the loan amount.

disintegration — the phase when a property's usefulness is in decline and constant upkeep is necessary.

divided agency — an agency in which the agent represents both the seller and the buyer without obtaining the consent of both.

documentary transfer tax — a tax imposed by counties and cities on the transfer of real property within their jurisdictions.

dominant tenement — land that is benefited by an easement appurtenant.

dormer — a projecting structure built out from a sloping roof that is used to provide windows and additional headroom for the upper floor.

drywall — prefabricated sheets or panels nailed to studs to form an interior wall or partition.

dual agent — a real estate broker who represents both the seller and the buyer in a real estate transaction.

due diligence — the exercise of an honest and reasonable degree of care in performing one's duties or obligations. A real estate agent's due diligence involves investigating the property to ensure that the property is as represented by the seller and to disclose accurate and complete information regarding the property.

due-on-sale clause — a clause in the promissory note, the security instrument, or both that states that the lender has the right to accelerate the loan if the secured property is sold or some other interest in the property is transferred.

duress — unlawful force or confinement used to compel a person to enter into a contract against his or her will.

DVA — the California Department of Veterans Affairs is a California state agency whose mission is to promote and deliver benefits to military veterans and their families who live in California.

dwelling house homestead — an automatic homestead.

earnest money deposit — a deposit that accompanies an offer by a buyer and is generally held in the broker's trust account.

easement — a non-possessory right to use a portion of another property owner's land for a specific purpose, as for a right-of-way, without paying rent or being considered a trespasser.

easement appurtenant — an easement that benefits, and is appurtenant to, another's land.

easement by necessity —arises as a creation of a court of law in certain cases were justice so demands, as in the case where a buyer of a parcel of land discovers that the land he or she just purchased has no access except over the land of someone other than from the person from whom the parcel was purchased.

easement in gross — an easement that benefits a legal person rather than other land.

Easton v. Strassburger — the 1984 landmark California court case that held that real estate agents have an "affirmative duty to conduct a reasonably competent and diligent inspection of the residential property listed for sale and to disclose to prospective purchasers all facts materially affecting the value of the property that such an investigation would reveal."

eaves — the overhang of a roof that projects over an exterior wall of a house.

economic life — the period of time that the property is useful or profitable to the average owner or investor.

economic obsolescence — *see*, external obsolescence.

EER and SEER — Air-conditioners have an efficiency rating that states the ratio of the cooling capacity (how many BTUs per hour) to the power drawn (in watts). For room air conditioners the ratio is the EER (energy efficiency ratio); for central air conditioners the rating is the SEER (seasonal energy efficiency ratio). The higher the EER or SEER, the greater the efficiency of the air-conditioning unit. Significant savings in electricity costs can be obtained by installing more efficient air-conditioning units.

effective age — the age of an improvement that is indicated by the condition of the improvement, as distinct from its chronological age.

effective demand — demand coupled with purchasing power sufficient to acquire the property from a willing seller in a free market.

effective gross income — income from a property after an allowance for vacancies and uncollectible rents is deducted from gross income.

ejectment — a legal action to recover possession of real property from a person who is not legally entitled to possess it, such as to remove an encroachment or to evict a defaulting buyer or tenant.

eLicensing — a system developed by the CalBRE that allows the examination application and the licensing process to be completed online.

emancipated minor — a minor who, because of marriage, military service, or court order, is allowed to contract for the sale or purchase of real property.

emblements — growing crops, such as grapes, avocados, and apples, that are produced seasonally through a tenant farmer's labor and industry.

eminent domain — right of the state to take, through due process proceedings (often referred to as *condemnation proceedings*), private property for public use upon payment of just compensation.

employee — a person who works for another who directs and controls the services rendered by the person.

employer — a person who directs and controls the services rendered by an employee.

encroachment — a thing affixed under, on, or above the land of another without permission.

encumber — To place a lien or other encumbrance on property.

encumbrance — A right or interest held by someone other than the owner the property that affects or limits the ownership of the property, such as easements and liens.

Endangered Species Act — a federal law that is intended to provide a means whereby the ecosystems upon which endangered species and threatened species depend may be conserved, and to provide a program for the conservation of such endangered species and threatened species.

environmental impact report (EIR) — a report that the agency investigating the feasibility of a development project pursuant to the California Environmental Quality Act is required to make if it is determined that there is substantial evidence of the project would have a significant adverse environmental impact.

environmental impact statement (EIS) — a statement that certain agencies are required to make pursuant to the National Environmental Policy Act regarding development that might significantly impact the quality of the environment.

Equal Credit Opportunity Act (ECOA) — a federal law that prohibits a lender from discriminating against any applicant for credit on the basis of race, color, religion, national origin, sex, marital status, or age (unless a minor), or on the grounds that some of the applicant's income derives from a public assistance program.

equal dignities rule — a principle of agency law that requires the same formality to create the agency as is required for the act(s) the agent is hired to perform.

equilibrium — the period of stability when the property changes very little.

equitable title — the right to possess and enjoy a property while the property is being paid for.

escalator clause — a provision in a lease that provides for periodic increases in rent, often based on the Consumer Price Index.

escheat — a process whereby property passes to the state if a person owning the property dies intestate without heirs.

escrow — a neutral depository in which something of value is held by an impartial third party (called the escrow agent) until all conditions specified in the escrow instructions have been fully performed.

escrow activity report — a report that certain real estate brokers must file with the CalBRE if their escrow activities exceed a certain threshold.

escrow agent — an impartial agent who holds possession of written instruments and deposits until all of the conditions of escrow have been fully performed.

escrow holder — an escrow agent

escrow instructions — the written instructions signed by all of the principals to the escrow (buyers, sellers, and lenders) that specify all of the conditions that must be met before the escrow agent may release whatever was deposited into escrow to the rightful parties.

estate — the degree, quantity, nature, duration, or extent of interest one has in real property.

estate at sufferance — a leasehold that arises when a lessee who legally obtained possession of a property remains on the property after the termination of the lease without the owner's consent. Such a holdover tenant can be evicted like a trespasser, but if the owner accepts rent, the estate automatically becomes a periodic tenancy.

estate at will — a leasehold that has no specified duration, though it may only be terminated by the owner of the property upon giving proper notice. An estate at will arises when a tenant takes possession of a property while negotiating a lease or under a void contract or lease.

estate for years — a leasehold that continues for a definite fixed period of time, measured in days, months, or years.

estate from period to period — a leasehold that continues from period to period, whether by days, months, or years, until terminated by proper notice.

estate of inheritance — a freehold estate.

estoppel — a legal principle that bars one from alleging or denying a fact because of one's own previous actions or words to the contrary. Ostensible agency can be created by estoppel when a principal and an unauthorized agent act in a manner toward a third-party that leads the third party to rely on the actions of the unauthorized agent, believing that the actions are authorized by the principal.

exclusive agency listing — a listing agreement that gives a broker the right to sell property and receive compensation (usually a commission) if the property is sold by anyone other than the owner of the property during the term of the listing.

exclusive authorization and right to sell listing — a listing agreement that gives a broker the exclusive right to sell property and receive compensation (usually a commission) if the property is sold by anyone, including the owner of the property, during the term of the listing.

executed contract— a contract that has been fully performed; may also refer to a contract that has been signed by all of the parties to the contract.

executor — a person named in a will to carry out the directions contained in the will.

executory contract — a contract that has not yet been fully performed by one or both parties.

express contract — a contract stated in words, written or oral.

external obsolescence — depreciation that results from things such as (1) changes in zoning laws or other government restrictions, (2) proximity to undesirable influences such as traffic, airport flight patterns, or power lines, and (3) general neighborhood deterioration, as might result from increased crime.

Factory Built Housing Law — a California state law that regulates factory built housing.

factory-built home — a home specifically manufactured to conform to the local building codes of the site, transported on flatbed trucks rather than being built on a permanent chassis, and assembled on the site where it is affixed it to a permanent foundation.

Fair Employment and Housing Act — a California state law (also known as the Rumford Act) that prohibits discrimination in the sale, leasing, or financing of nearly all types of housing, except the rental to one boarder in a single-family, owner-occupied home or to accommodations operated by charitable, fraternal, or religious organizations. The Rumford Act specifically prohibits landlords from asking prospective buyers or tenants about race, color, religion, gender, sexual orientation, marital status, familial status, national origin, ancestry, or disability.

Fair Housing Act — *see*, Civil Rights Act of 1968

false promise — a promise made without any intention of performing it.

Fannie Mae — a U.S. government conservatorship originally created as the Federal National Mortgage Association in 1938 to purchase mortgages from primary lenders.

federally designated targeted area — federally designated locations where homeownership is encouraged and incentivized.

fee simple absolute estate — the greatest estate that the law permits in land. The owner of a fee simple absolute estate owns all present and future interests in the property.

fee simple defeasible estate — a fee estate that is qualified by some condition that, if violated, may "defeat" the estate and lead to its loss and reversion to the grantor.

FHA — the Federal Housing Administration is a federal agency that was created by the National Housing Act of 1934 in order to make housing more affordable by increasing home construction, reducing unemployment, and making home mortgages more available and affordable.

FHFA — the Federal Housing Finance Agency is a U.S. government agency created by the Housing and Economic Recovery Act of 2008 to oversee the activities of Fannie Mae and Freddie Mac in order to strengthen the secondary mortgage market.

FICO score — a credit score created by the Fair Isaac Corporation that ranges from 300 to 850 and is used by lenders to help evaluate the creditworthiness of a potential borrower.

fiduciary relationship — a relationship in which one owes a duty of utmost care, integrity, honesty, and loyalty to another.

final map —a final map that a planning commission must approve after consideration of a tentative map before regulated subdivided property may be sold.

final public report — a report that the Real Estate Commissioner issues after determining that a subdivision offering meets certain consumer protection standards.

finder — a person who merely introduces a buyer to a seller, but does nothing else to facilitate a transaction between the buyer and seller, such as rendering assistance in negotiating terms.

fire stop — a block or board placed horizontally between studs to form a tight closure of a concealed space, thereby decreasing drafts and retarding the spread of fire and smoke.

first mortgage — a security instrument that holds first-priority claim against certain property identified in the instrument.

fiscal year — in California, the fiscal year begins on July 1 and ends on June 30 of the following calendar year.

fixed lease — a gross lease

fixture — an object, originally personal property, that is attached to the land in such a manner as to be considered real property.

flashing — sheet metal or other material used in roof and wall construction to prevent water from entering.

flue — a channel in a chimney through which flame and smoke passes upward to the outer air.

footing — concrete poured on solid ground that provides support for the foundation, chimney, or support columns. Footing should be placed below the frost line to prevent movement.

foreclosure — a legal process by which a lender, in an attempt to recover the balance of a loan from a borrower who has defaulted on the loan, forces the sale of the collateral that secured the loan.

foreclosure consultant — any person who makes any solicitation, representation, or offer to any owner to perform for compensation or who, for compensation, performs any service which the person in any manner represents will in any manner stop or postpone the foreclosure sale; obtain any forbearance from any beneficiary or mortgagee; assist the owner to exercise the right of reinstatement; obtain any extension of the period within which the owner may reinstate his or her obligation; obtain any waiver of an acceleration clause contained in any promissory note or contract secured by a deed of trust or mortgage on a residence in foreclosure or contained that deed of trust or mortgage; assist the owner to obtain a loan or advance of funds; avoid or ameliorate the impairment of the owner's credit resulting from the recording of a notice of default or the conduct of a foreclosure sale; save the owner's residence from foreclosure; or assist the owner in obtaining from the beneficiary, mortgagee, trustee under a power of sale, or counsel for the beneficiary, mortgagee, or trustee, the remaining proceeds from the foreclosure sale of the owner's residence. Exempted from the definition of foreclosure consultant are licensed attorneys who render foreclosure consultant services to clients in the course of his or her practice as an attorney, licensed real estate brokers, and licensed real estate salespersons who work under the supervision of their employing broker.

foreclosure prevention alternative — a first lien loan modification or another available loss mitigation option.

Foreign Investment in Real Property Tax Act (FIRPTA) — a federal act that, with certain exceptions, requires the buyer in a real estate transaction to determine whether the seller is a non-resident alien; and if so, the buyer has the responsibility of withholding 10% of the amount realized from the sale and sending that 10% of the IRS.

Form Report — *see*, Summary Report.

four unities — refers to the common law rule that a joint tenancy requires unity of possession, time, interest, and title.

Freddie Mac — a U.S. government conservatorship originally created as the Federal Home Loan Mortgage Corporation in 1968 to purchase mortgages from primary lenders.

freehold estate — an estate in land whereby the holder of the estate owns rights in the property for an indefinite duration.

front-end ratio — the ratio of monthly housing expenses to monthly gross income.

fully amortized loan — a loan whereby the installment payments are sufficient to pay off the entire loan by the end of the loan term.

fully indexed rate — on an adjustable-rate mortgage, the index plus the margin.

functional obsolescence — depreciation that results (1) from deficiencies arising from poor architectural design, out-dated style or equipment, and changes in utility demand, such as for larger houses with more garage space, or (2) from over-improvements, where the cost of the improvements was more than the addition to market value.

gable roof — a roof with two sloping sides but not sloping ends.

gambrel roof — a roof sloped on two sides, each side having a steep lower slope and a flatter upper slope.

Garn-St. Germain Act — a federal law that made enforceability of due-on-sale provisions a federal issue.

general agent — an agent who is authorized by a principal to act for more than a particular act or transaction. General agents are usually an integral part of an ongoing business enterprise.

general lien — a lien that attaches to all of a person's nonexempt property.

general partnership — a partnership in which each partner has the equal right to manage the partnership and has personal liability for all of the partnership debts.

general plan — a comprehensive, long-term plan for the physical development of a city or county that is implemented by zoning, building codes, and other laws or actions of the local governments.

gift deed — a deed used to convey title when no tangible consideration (other than "affection") is given. The gift deed is valid unless it was used to defraud creditors, in which case such creditors may bring an action to void the deed.

Ginnie Mae — the Government National Mortgage Association is a wholly owned U.S. government corporation within HUD to guarantee pools of eligible loans that primary lenders issue as Ginnie Mae mortgage-backed securities.

good-faith improver — a person who, because of a mistake of law or fact, makes an improvement to land in good faith and under erroneous belief that he or she is the owner of the land.

goodwill — an intangible asset derived from the expectation of continued public patronage.

graduated lease — a lease that is similar to a gross lease except that it provides for periodic increases in rent, often based on the Consumer Price Index.

grant deed — the deed most commonly used in California. It has two implied warranties that are enforced whether or not they are expressly stated in the deed: the grantor has not transferred title to anyone else, and the property at the time of execution is free from any encumbrances made by the grantor, except for those disclosed.

grantee — one who acquires an interest in real property from another.

grantor — one who transfers an interest in real property to another.

gross income — total income from a property before any expenses are deducted.

gross income multiplier (GIM) — a number equal to the estimated value of a property divided by the gross income of the property.

gross lease — a lease under which the tenant pays a fixed rental amount, and the landlord pays all of the operating expenses for the premises.

gross rent multiplier (GRM) — a number equal to the estimated value of a property divided by the gross rental income of the property.

ground lease — a lease under which a tenant leases land and agrees to construct a building or to make other significant improvements on the land.

group action — in antitrust law, two or more persons agreeing to act in a certain way.

group boycott — in antitrust law, the action of two or more brokers agreeing not to deal with another broker or brokers.

heir — a person entitled to obtain property through intestate succession.

hip roof — a sloping roof that rises from all four sides of the house.

Holden Act — *see*, Housing Financial Discrimination Act.

holographic will — a will written, dated, and signed by a testator in his or her own handwriting.

home equity line of credit (HELOC) — a revolving line of credit provided by a home equity mortgage.

home equity mortgage — a security instrument used to provide the borrower with a revolving line of credit based on the amount of equity in the borrower's home.

homeowner's exemption — and exemption of $7,000 from the assessed value of a homeowner's residence.

Homeowner's Protection Act (HPA) — a federal law that requires lenders to disclose to borrowers when the borrowers' mortgages no longer require PMI.

homestead declaration —a recorded document that claims a particular dwelling (such as a house, condominium, boat, or mobile home) as the owner's principal place of residence and that provides limited protection for the claimant's equity in the dwelling.

homestead exemption — the amount of a homeowner's equity that may be protected from unsecured creditors.

Housing Financial Discrimination Act — a California state law (also referred to as the Holden Act) that prohibits redlining by making it illegal for financial institutions to consider the racial, ethnic, national origin, or religious composition of a neighborhood when determining whether to make loans or to provide financial assistance for housing in that neighborhood.

HUD-1 Uniform Settlement Statement — an escrow settlement form mandated by RESPA for use in all escrows pertaining to the purchase of owner-occupied residences of 1-4 dwelling units that use funds from institutional lenders regulated by the federal government.

implication — the act of creating an agency relationship by an unauthorized agent who acts as if he or she is the agent of a principal, and this principal reasonably believes that the unauthorized agent is acting as his or her actual agent.

implied contract— a contract not expressed in words, but, through action or inaction, understood by the parties.

implied easement — an easement arising by implication, as when a purchaser of mineral rights automatically acquires an implied right to enter the property to extract the minerals.

impound account — *see*, reserve account

Improvement Bond Act of 1915 — this act permits local governments to issue bonds to finance subdivision street improvements. Owners of the subdivisions bear the cost of redeeming the bonds.

inclusionary zoning — a zoning law that requires builders to set aside a specific portion of new construction for people of low to moderate incomes.

income approach — an appraisal approach that estimates the value of an income-producing property as being worth the present value of the future income of the property through a three-step process: (1) determine the net annual income, (2) determine an appropriate capitalization rate, and (3) divide the net income by the capitalization rate to obtain the estimate of value.

incurable depreciation — depreciation that results from (1) physical deterioration or functional obsolescence that cannot be repaired at a cost that is less than or equal to the value added to the property and (2) economic obsolescence (which is beyond the control of the property owner).

independent contractor — a person who performs work for someone, but does so independently in a private trade, business, or profession, with little or no supervision from the person for whom the work is performed.

index — under an adjustable-rate mortgage, a benchmark rate of interest that is adjusted periodically according to the going rate of T-bills, LIBOR, or the like.

individual building manager — a property manager who usually manages just a single large property.

individual property manager — a real estate broker who manages properties for one or more property owners.

installment note — a promissory note in which periodic payments are made, usually consisting of interest due and some repayment of principal.

installment sale — a sale in which the seller receives at least one payment in a later tax period and may report part of the gain from the sale for the year in which a payment is received.

integration — the growth and development stage of property.

interest — the compensation allowed by law or fixed by the parties for the use, or forbearance, or detention of money.

interest-rate cap —under an adjustable-rate mortgage, the maximum that the interest rate can increase from one adjustment period to the next or over the life of the entire loan.

interpleader — an action that allows for a neutral third party (such as a real estate agent) to avoid liability to two or more claimants (such as a seller and buyer) to the same money or property (such as an earnest money deposit) by forcing the claimants to litigate among themselves, letting the court determine who deserves what while not enmeshing the neutral third party in the litigation.

Interstate Land Sales Full Disclosure Act — a federal consumer protection act that requires that certain land developers register with the Bureau of Consumer Financial Protection if they offer across state lines parcels in subdivisions containing 100 or more lots. A regulated developer must provide each prospective buyer with a Property Report that contains pertinent information about the subdivision and that discloses to the prospective buyer that he or she has a minimum of 7 days in which to cancel a purchase agreement.

intestate — not having made, or not having disposed of by, a will.

intestate succession — transfer of the property of one who dies intestate.

involuntary lien — a lien created by operation of law, not by the voluntary acts of the debtor.

jamb — the vertical sides of a door or window that contact the door or sash.

joint ownership — ownership of property by two or more persons.

joint tenancy —a form of joint ownership which has unity of possession, time, interest, and title.

joist — one of a series of parallel heavy horizontal timbers used to support floor or ceiling loads.

Jones v. Mayer — a landmark 1968 United States Supreme Court case that held that the Civil Rights Act of 1866 was constitutional and that the Act prohibited all racial discrimination, whether private or public, in the sale or rental of property.

judicial foreclosure — a foreclosure carried out not by way of a power-of-sale clause in a security instrument, but under the supervision of a court.

judgment — a court's final determination of the rights and duties of the parties in an action before it.

jumbo loan — a mortgage loan the amount of which exceeds conforming loan limits set by the FHFA on an annual basis.

junior mortgage — a mortgage that, relative to another mortgage, has a lower lien-priority position.

land contract — a real property sales contract.

land installment contract — a real property sales contract.

lateral support — the support that soil receives from the land adjacent to it.

lease extension — a continuation of tenancy under the original lease.

lease renewal — a continuation of tenancy under a new lease.

leasehold estate — a less-than-freehold estate.

legatee — one who acquires personal property under a will.

lessee — a person (the tenant) who leases property from another.

lessor — a person (the landlord) who leases property to another.

less-than-freehold estate — an estate in which the holder has the exclusive right to possession of land for a length of time. The holder of a less-than-freehold estate is usually referred to as a lessee or tenant.

level payment note — a promissory note under which all periodic installment payments are equal.

leverage — a method of multiplying gains or losses on investments, usually by using borrowed money to acquire the investments.

license to use —a personal right to use property on a nonexclusive basis. A license to use is not considered an estate.

lien —an encumbrance against real property that is used to secure a debt and that can, in most cases, be foreclosed.

lien priority — the order in which lien holders are paid.

lien stripping — a method sometimes used in Chapter 13 bankruptcies to eliminate junior liens on the debtor's home.

life estate — a freehold estate the duration of which is measured by the life of a natural person — either by the life of the person holding the estate, or by the life or lives of one or more other persons.

limited liability partnership — a partnership in which there is at least one general partner and one or more limited partners. The limited partners have no liability beyond their investment in and pledges to the partnership.

lintel — a horizontal support made of wood, stone, concrete, or steal that lies across the top of a window or door and supports the load above.

liquidated damages — a sum of money that the parties agree, usually at the formation of a contract, will serve as the exact amount of damages that will be paid upon a breach of the contract.

lis pendens — (Latin for "action pending") a notice of pendency of action.

listing agreement — a written contract between a real estate broker and a property owner (the principal) stipulating that in exchange for the real estate broker's procuring a buyer for the principal's property, the principal will compensate the broker, usually with a percentage of the selling price.

loan modification — a restructuring or modification of a mortgage or deed of trust on terms more favorable to the buyer's ability (or desire) to continue making loan payments.

loan servicing — the administration of a loan from the time the loan proceeds are dispersed to the time the loan is paid off in full.

loan-to-value ratio (LTV) — the amount of a first mortgage divided by the lesser of (1) the appraised value of the property or (2) the purchase price of the property.

long-term capital gain — the capital gain on the sale of a capital asset that was held for a relatively long period of time, usually more than one year.

lot, block, and tract land description — (see "recorded map land description")

maker — the person who makes a promissory note.

manufactured home — a structure that was constructed on or after June 15, 1976 and built to HUD standards; transportable in one or more sections; eight body feet or more in width, or 40 body feet or more in length, in the traveling mode, or, when erected on site, is 320 or more square feet; built on a permanent chassis.

margin — a number of percentage points, usually fixed over the life of the loan, that is added to the index of an adjustable-rate mortgage to arrive at the fully indexed rate.

market allocation — in antitrust law, the process of competitors agreeing to divide up geographic areas or types of products or services they offer to customers.

market price — the price actually paid for a particular property.

market value — as defined for appraisal purposes by HUD/FHA is: "The most probable price which a property should bring in a competitive and open market under all conditions requisite to a fair sale, the buyer and seller, each acting prudently, knowledgeably and assuming the price is not affected by undue stimulus."

material fact — a fact that is likely to affect the decision of a party as to whether to enter into a transaction on the specified terms.

mechanics lien — a specific lien claimed by someone who furnished labor or materials for a work of improvement on real property and who has not been fully paid.

Megan's Law — a law that provides for the registration of sex offenders and for the making available to the public information regarding the location of these offenders.

Mello-Roos Community Facilities Act — this act provides for the construction or improvement of a wide variety of facilities and services. Because the property tax burden on Mello-Roos districts can be quite high, a seller of a residential structure consisting of 4 or fewer dwellings that is subject to a lien of a Mello-Roos district must make a good-faith effort to obtain from the district a disclosure notice concerning the special assessment and give notice of the disclosure to prospective purchasers.

menace — a threat to commit duress or to commit injury to person or property.

meridians — (see and compare "base lines")

metes and bounds land description — a method of describing a parcel of land that uses physical features of the locale, along with directions and distances, to define the boundaries of the parcel.

minor — in California, a person who is under 18 years of age.

mobile home — a structure that was constructed before June 15, 1976; transportable in one or more sections; eight body feet or more in width, or 40 body feet or more in length, in the traveling mode, or, when erected on site, is 320 or more square feet; built on a permanent chassis.

mobile home park — an area of land where two or more mobile home sites are rented, or held out for rent, to accommodate mobile homes used for human habitation.

moldings — patterned strips, usually of wood, used to provide ornamental finish to cornices, bases, windows, and door jambs.

mortgage banker — a primary lender that uses its own money in creating a mortgage loan.

mortgage broker — an individual or company that finds borrowers and matches them with lenders for a fee.

mortgagee — a lender or creditor to whom a mortgagor gives a mortgage to secure a loan or performance of an obligation.

Mortgage Forgiveness Debt Relief Act of 2007 — a federal law that allowed taxpayers to exclude from income debt that is canceled on their principal residence (not on a second home) through foreclosure, loan modification, or other form of debt cancellation. The amount of canceled debt that can be excluded from income is $2 million for a married couple filing jointly, or $1 million for individuals or married persons filing separately. After being extended several times, this Act expired at the end of 2013.

mortgage loan originator (MLO) — a person who takes, or offers to take, a residential mortgage loan application or offers or negotiates terms of a residential mortgage application for compensation or gain or in expectation of compensation or gain.

mortgagor — the borrower who gives a mortgage on his or her property to secure a loan or performance of an obligation.

mudsill — for houses built on a concrete slab, the wood sills that are bolted to all sides of the slab, providing a means of attaching portions of the framing for the house to the foundation.

multiple listing service — an organization (MLS) of real estate brokers who share their listings with other members of the organization.

mutual consent — refers to the situation in which all parties to a contract freely agree to the terms of the contract; sometimes referred to as a "meeting of the minds."

Narrative Report — *see*, Self-Contained Report.

National "Do Not Call" Registry — a registry established by the Federal Trade Commission to protect consumers from unwanted commercial telephone solicitations.

National Association of Real Estate Brokers — a real estate trade association whose members are called Realtists®.

National Association of Realtors® — the largest real estate trade association in the United States, founded in 1908, whose members are called Realtors®.

National Environmental Policy Act (NEPA) — a federal law intended to protect, and to promote the enhancement of, the environment.

negative amortization — a loan repayment scheme in which the outstanding principal balance of the loan increases because the installment payments do not cover the full interest due.

negative amortized loan (NegAm loan) — a loan by which the installment payments do not cover all of the interest due — the unpaid part of the interest due being tacked onto the principal, thereby causing the principal to grow as each month goes by.

negative declaration — a report issued by a state or local agency acting pursuant to the California Environmental Quality Act if the agency determines that a development project will not have a significant adverse environmental impact.

negative fraud — the act of not disclosing a material fact which induces someone to enter into a contractual relationship and that causes that person damage or loss.

net income — income from a property remaining after expenses are deducted from gross income.

net lease — a lease under which the tenant pays a fixed rental amount plus some of the landlord's operating expenses.

net listing — a listing agreement providing the broker with all proceeds received from the sale over a specified amount.

NMLS — the Nationwide Mortgage Licensing System and Registry is a mortgage licensing system developed and maintained by the Conference of State Bank Supervisors and the American Association of Residential Mortgage Regulators for the state licensing and registration of state-licensed loan originators.

nonconforming loan — a loan not in conformance with FHFA guidelines.

nonconforming use — a zoning exception for areas that are zoned for the first time or that are rezoned and where established property uses that previously were permitted to not conform to the new zoning requirements. As a general rule, such existing properties are "grandfathered in," allowing them to continue the old use but not to extend the old use to additional properties or to continue the old use after rebuilding or abandonment.

non-judicial foreclosure — a foreclosure process culminating in a privately conducted, publicly held trustee's sale. The right to pursue a non-judicial foreclosure is contained in the power-of-sale clause of a mortgage or deed of trust, which, upon borrower default and the beneficiary's request, empowers the trustee to sell the secured property at a public auction.

notice of cessation — a written form that notifies that all work of improvement on a piece of real property has ceased, and that limits the time in which mechanics liens may be filed against the property.

notice of completion — a written form that notifies that a work of improvement on real property has been completed, and that limits the time in which mechanics liens may be filed against the property.

notice of default (NOD) — a document prepared by a trustee at the direction of a lender to begin a non-judicial foreclosure proceeding.

notice of nonresponsibility — a written notice that a property owner may record and post on the property to shield the owner from any liability for a work of improvement on the property that a lessee or a purchaser under a land sales contract authorized.

notice of pendency of action — a notice that provides constructive notice to potential purchasers or encumbrancers of a piece of real property of the pendency of a lawsuit in which an interest in that piece of real property is claimed.

notice of sale — a document prepared by a trustee at the direction of a lender that gives notice of the time and place of sale of an identified foreclosed property.

novation — a substitution of a new obligation or contract for an old one, or the substitution of one party to a contract by another, relieving the original party of liability under the contract.

nuisance — anything that is indecent or offensive to the senses, or an obstruction to the free use of property, so as to interfere with the comfortable enjoyment of life or property.

nuncupative will — an oral will; nuncupative wills are no longer valid in California.

offer — a proposal by one person (the offeror) to enter into a contract with another (the offeree).

offeree — one to whom an offer to enter into a contract is made.

offeror — one who makes an offer to enter into a contract.

open listing — a listing agreement that gives a broker the nonexclusive right to sell property and receive compensation (usually a commission) if, but only if, the broker is the first to procure a buyer for the property.

option contract — a contract that gives the purchaser of the option the right to buy or lease a certain property at a set price any time during the option term.

option listing — a listing agreement in which the broker is given the right to sell the subject property or to purchase it at a specified price for a specified time.

ordinary interest — interest calculated by the 30/360 day count convention.

ostensible agency — an agency in which the principal intentionally, or by want of ordinary care, causes a third person to believe another to be his agent who was not actually employed by him.

parol evidence rule — a rule that prohibits the introduction of extrinsic evidence of preliminary negotiations, oral or written, and of contemporaneous oral evidence, to alter the terms of a written agreement that appears to be whole.

partial release clause — a clause in a blanket mortgage that allows a developer to sell off individual parcels and pay back, according to a release schedule, only a proportionate amount of the blanket loan.

partition —a court-ordered or voluntary division of real property held in joint ownership into parcels owned in severalty.

passive income — in general, income from either rental activity or from a business in which the taxpayer does not materially participate.

passive investor — an investor who does not actively contribute to the management of the business invested in.

patent, land — an instrument used to convey government land.

payee — the person to whom a promissory note is made out.

payment cap —under an adjustable-rate mortgage, the maximum amount that installment payments may increase from one adjustment period to the next or over the life of the loan.

percentage lease — a lease, often used in shopping centers, under which the tenant typically pays a base rent amount plus a percentage of the gross receipts of the tenant's business.

period of redemption — a period of time after a sheriff's sale in a judicial foreclosure proceeding during which the borrower may redeem his or her property by paying off the entire debt plus costs.

periodic tenancy — an estate from period to period.

physical deterioration — depreciation that results from wear and tear of use and from natural causes.

physical life — the period of time that the property lasts with normal maintenance.

pitch — the degree of inclination or slope of a roof.

plaintiff — the one who brings a lawsuit.

planned development (PD) — a development (other than a condominium, community apartment project, or stock cooperative) consisting of lots or parcels owned separately and areas owned in common and reserved for the use of some or all the owners of the separate interests.

planning commission — the city or county agency responsible for proposing a general plan for the city or county.

plaster — a mixture of lime or gypsum, sand, water, and fiber that is applied to walls and ceilings and that hardens into a smooth coating.

point of beginning — the fixed starting point in the metes and bounds method of land description.

points — see discount points.

police power — the power of a government to impose restrictions on private rights, including property rights, for the sake of public welfare, health, order, and security, for which no compensation need be made.

portfolio loans — loans that primary lenders retain in their own investment portfolios rather than sell into the secondary market.

post-dated check — a check dated with a date after the date the check is written and signed.

power of attorney — a special written instrument that gives authority to an agent to conduct certain business on behalf of the principal. The agent acting under such a grant is sometimes called an attorney in fact.

power-of-sale clause — a clause contained in most trust deeds that permits the trustee to foreclose on, and sell, the secured property without going to court.

preapproval —an evaluation of a potential borrower's ability to qualify for a loan that involves a credit check and verification of income and debt of the potential borrower.

preliminary notice — a notice sent by someone who furnishes work or materials for a work of improvement on real property that creates a right to file a mechanics lien against the property.

preliminary public report — a report that a subdivider may request that requires fewer disclosures than does a final public report and that only allows the subdivider to accept reservations from potential purchasers.

preliminary title report — a statement by a title insurance company of the condition of the title and of the terms and conditions upon which the company is willing to issue a policy.

prepayment penalty — a fee charged to a borrower for paying off the loan faster than scheduled payments call for.

prequalification — an initial unverified evaluation of a potential borrower's ability to qualify for a mortgage loan.

prescription — a method of acquiring an interest in property by use and enjoyment for five years.

prescriptive easement — an easement acquired by prescription.

price fixing — an agreement between competitors to set prices or price ranges.

primary financing — first mortgage property financing.

primary lender — lenders who originate mortgage loans.

primary mortgage market — the market where mortgage loans are originated.

principal — the one whom an agent represents.

principle of anticipation — principle that value is derived from a calculation of anticipated future benefits to be derived from the property, not from past benefits, though past benefits may inform as to what might be expected in the future.

principle of balance — principle that the maximum value of property, its highest and best use, is created and maintained when land use by interacting elements of production are in equilibrium or balance.

principle of change — principle that property values are in a constant state of flux due to economic, environmental, political, social, and physical forces in the area.

principle of competition — principle that increased competition results in increased supply in relation to demand, and thereby to lower profit margins.

principle of conformity — principle that the maximum value of land is achieved when there is a reasonable degree of social, economic, and architectural conformity in the area.

principle of contribution — principle that improvements made to a property will contribute to its value or that, conversely, the lack of a needed improvement will detract from the value of the property.

principle of four-stage life cycle — principle that property goes through a process of growth, stability, decline, and revitalization.

principle of progression — principle that the value of a residence of less value tends to be enhanced by proximity to residences of higher value.

principle of regression — principle that the value of a residence of higher value tends to be degraded by the proximity to residences of lower value.

principle of substitution — principle that the value of a property will tend toward the cost of an equally desirable substitute property.

principle of supply and demand — principle that the value of property in a competitive market is influenced by the relative levels of supply and demand: the greater level of demand in relation to the level of supply, the greater the value.

principle of the highest and best use — principle that the best use of a property in terms of value is the use most likely to produce the greatest net return (in terms of money or other valued items).

private mortgage insurance (PMI) — mortgage insurance that lenders often require for loans with an LTV more than 80%.

privity of contract — a legal doctrine that states that a legally enforceable relationship exists between the persons who are parties to a contract.

privity of estate — a legal doctrine that states that a legally enforceable relationship exists between the parties who hold interests in the same real property.

probate — a legal procedure whereby a superior court in the county where the real property is located or where the deceased resided oversees the distribution of the decedent's property.

profit á prendre — the right to enter another's land for such purposes as to drill for oil, mine for coal, or cut and remove timber.

promissory note — a contract whereby one person unconditionally promises to pay another a certain sum of money, either at a fixed or determinable future date or on demand of the payee.

property tax postponement program — a program in which the state pays all or part of the real property tax on a qualified senior's residence until he or she moves, sells the property, dies, or transfers title to the property. Repayment of all postponed taxes must be paid when the property is sold or title transferred.

Proposition 13 — an amendment to the California state Constitution that places a maximum ad valorem tax on real property equal to 1% of the "full cash value" plus a maximum increase of the assessed value of up to 2% per year, as long as the annual increase does not exceed the Consumer Price Index for that year.

Proposition 193 — this law extends Proposition 58 tax relief to certain transfers from grandparents to their grandchildren, but not transfers from grandchildren to their grandparents.

Proposition 58 — this law provides for an exclusion from reassessment when property is transferred between spouses. It also provides for an exclusion from reassessment of a transfer of a principal residence and transfers of the first $1 million of other real property between parent and child.

Proposition 60 — this law allows certain older persons to transfer the adjusted basis of their present principal residence to a replacement if the replacement is in the same county and is of equal or lesser value than the prior residence.

Proposition 8 — this law requires the county assessor to assess real property either at the property's Proposition 13 adjusted value or its current market value, whichever is less.

Proposition 90 — this law extends Proposition 60 to allow the purchase of a new residence in a different California county, but only if the county in which the new residence lies adopts Proposition 90.

proration — an adjustment of expenses that either have been paid or are in arrears in proportion to actual time of ownership as of the closing of escrow or other agreed-upon date.

public dedication — a gift of an interest in land to a public body for public use, such as for a street, a park, or an easement to access a beach.

public grant — public land conveyed, usually for a small fee, to individuals or to organizations, such as to railroads or universities.

puffing — the act of expressing a positive opinion about something to induce someone to become a party to a contract.

purchase money loan — a deed of trust or mortgage on a dwelling for not more than four families given to a lender to secure repayment of a loan which was in fact used to pay all or part of the purchase price of that dwelling, occupied entirely or in part by the purchaser.

pyramid roof — a hip roof that has no ridge.

quitclaim deed — a deed that contains no warranties of any kind, no after-acquired title provisions, and provides the grantee with the least protection of any deed; it merely provides that any interest (if there is any) that the grantor has in the property is transferred to the grantee.

rafter — one of a series of parallel sloping timbers that extend from the ridgeboard to the exterior walls, providing support for the roof.

ratification — the act of creating an agency relationship by a principal who accepts or retains the benefit of an act made by an unauthorized agent.

Real Estate Commissioner — the chief executive officer of the CalBRE who is appointed by the governor and whose responsibility is to oversee and enforce the Real Estate Law and the Subdivided Lands Law and to issue regulations, known as the Regulations of the Real Estate Commissioner, that have the full force and effect of law.

Real Estate Fund — a special account controlled by the California State Treasury into which real estate license fees are deposited.

real estate investment trust (REIT) — a company that invests in and, in most cases operates, income-producing real estate and that meets numerous criteria, such as the necessity of being jointly owned by at least 100 persons.

real estate owned (REO) — property acquired by a lender through a foreclosure sale.

real estate professional — a real estate investor who (1) materially participates for at least 750 hours during the tax year in the real estate business and (2) spends more than 50% of his or her personal services performed in all businesses during the tax year in the real estate business that he or she materially participates in.

Real Estate Settlement Procedures Act (RESPA) — a federal law designed to prevent lenders, real estate agents, developers, title insurance companies, and other agents (such as appraisers and inspectors) who service the real estate settlement process from providing kickbacks or referral fees to each other, and from facilitating bait-and-switch tactics.

Real Estate Transfer Disclosure Statement"("TDS") — a form that a seller of a residential real estate property of 1 to 4 units must complete, sign, and have delivered to a buyer. The TDS must also be completed in part by the agent representing the seller, stating whatever defects are discovered or known by the agent.

Real Property Loans Act — a California law that addresses abuses and loan charges on small loans secured by real property.

real property sales contract — an agreement in which one party agrees to convey title to real property to another party upon the satisfaction of specified conditions set forth in the contract and that does not require conveyance of title within one year from the date of formation of the contract.

Realtist® — a member of the National Association of Real Estate Brokers.

Realtor® — a member of the National Association of Realtors®.

reconciliation — the process of ascertaining value by comparing and evaluating values obtained from comparables or from different valuation approaches; the process of comparing what is in a trust fund account with what should be in the account.

reconveyance deed — a deed executed by the trustee of a deed of trust after the promissory note is paid off in full by the borrower and the lender instructs the trustee to so execute the reconveyance deed, which reconveys legal title to the borrower

recorded map land description — a method of land description that states a property's lot, block, and tract number, referring to a map recorded in the county where the property is located.

Recovery Account — a special account into which is credited some of the funds from the Real Estate Fund, which funds are used to reimburse members of the public who have obtained a civil judgment or criminal restitution order against a real estate licensee but have not been able to collect fully from the licensee through normal collection efforts.

redemption period — a period of time extending for 3 months after a sheriff's sale if the proceeds of the sale is enough to pay off the debt and all costs of foreclosure; it is 1 year if the proceeds of the sale are not enough to pay off the debt *and* the lender pursues a deficiency judgment. If the lender elects not to pursue a deficiency judgment, there is no right of redemption.

redlining — the illegal practice of refusing to make loans for real property in particular areas.

Regulation Z — the set of regulations that implement the Truth-in-Lending Act (TILA).

reinforced concrete — concrete poured around steel bars or metal netting to increase its ability to withstand tensile, shear, and compression stresses.

rejection — the act of an offeree that terminates an offer. An offer may be rejected (1) by submitting a new offer, (2) by submitting what purports to be an acceptance but is not because it contains a variance of a material term of the original offer, or (3) by express terms of rejection.

rejuvenation — the phase when a property is rebuilt, remodeled, or otherwise revitalized to a new highest and best use.

reliction — a natural process by which the owner of riparian or littoral property acquires additional land that has been covered by water but has become permanently uncovered by the gradual recession of water.

remainder — the residue of a freehold estate where, at the end of the estate, the future interest arises in a third person.

remainder depreciation — depreciation that will occur after the date of valuation.

remainderman — a person who inherits or is entitled to inherit property held as a life estate when the person whose life determines the duration of the life estate passes away.

replacement cost — the cost of replacing improvements with those having equivalent utility, but constructed with modern materials, designs, and workmanship.

reproduction cost — the cost of replacing improvements with exact replicas at current prices.

request for a reconveyance — an instrument that a lender sends to a trustee requesting that the trustee execute and record a deed of reconveyance that is then sent to the borrower.

rescission — the cancellation of a contract and the restoration of each party to the same position held before the contract was entered into.

reserve account — in reference to loan servicing, the escrow account from which the loan servicer typically pays, on behalf of the borrower, property taxes, hazard insurance, and any other charges (such as mortgage insurance) with respect to the loan.

resident manager — an individual who resides on the premises, is a "responsible" person, and has "charge" of the apartment building.

residential loan — a loan primarily for personal, family, or household use secured by a residential structure that contains 1 to 4 dwelling units. The term also includes a loan for an individual condominium unit, cooperative unit, mobile home, manufactured home, and trailer, if it is used as a residence.

residual value — an estimate of the reasonable fair market value of a property at the end of its useful life.

respondeat superior — in agency law, the doctrine that a principal is liable for the acts of an agent if those acts were performed within the scope of the agent's authority. (See, vicarious liability.)

Restricted Use Report — a type of appraisal report that is sometimes used when the client is familiar with the area and a report summarizing the data that supports the final estimate of value is not necessary. The Restricted Use Report must contain a notice that it is to be used only by the client for one particular purpose, not by potential buyers or lenders or others.

retaliatory eviction — an eviction action brought to retaliate against a tenant for making a habitability complaint or for asserting other of the tenant's legal rights.

return on investment (ROI) — an investor's cash flow (net income minus financing charges) divided by the investor's actual cash investment (as distinct from the purchase price).

reverse mortgage — a security instrument for a loan for homeowners over the age of 62 who have a large amount of equity in their homes, usually designed to provide such homeowners with monthly payments, often over the lifetime of the last surviving homeowner who either moves out of the house or dies.

reversion — the residue of a freehold estate where at the end of the estate, the future interest reverts to the grantor.

revocation — the withdrawal of an offer by the person who made the offer.

rezoning amendment — an amendment to a zoning ordinance that property owners may request if they feel that their area has been improperly zoned.

ridgeboard — a horizontal board placed on edge at the apex of a roof to which the upper ends of the rafters are attached.

right of first refusal — the right to be given the first chance to purchase a property at the same price, terms, and conditions as is offered to third parties if and when the property is put up for sale.

right of reinstatement — a borrower's right to, at any time within the period from the date of recordation of the notice of default until 5 business days prior to the date of sale, have his or her loan reinstated by paying all delinquent loan installments, foreclosure costs, and trustee's fees. No right of reinstatement exists after a trustee's sale, when the purchaser immediately acquires all rights held by the former owner, subject to the rights of holders of rights superior to the mortgage that was foreclosed.

right of survivorship — the right to succeed to the interest of a joint tenant or, if community property with right of survivorship, to succeed to the interest of a spouse or registered domestic partner. Right of survivorship is the most important characteristic of joint tenancy.

riparian rights — the rights of a landowner to use water from a stream or lake adjacent to his or her property, provided such use is reasonable and does not injure other riparian owners.

Rumford Act — *see*, Fair Employment and Housing Act

R-value — a measure of the resistance of insulation to heat transfer. The FTC requires sellers of new homes to disclose the R-value of each home's insulation. The higher the R-value, the greater is the effectiveness of the insulation.

SAFE Act — the Safe and Fair Enforcement for Mortgage Licensing Act of 2008 was designed to improve consumer protection and reduce mortgage fraud by setting minimum standards for the licensing and registration of mortgage loan originators.

safety clause — a clause in a listing agreement that protects the broker's commission for a sale that is consummated after the termination of the broker's listing agreement to a buyer who is found by the broker during the term of the listing agreement.

sales comparison approach — an appraisal approach that compares recent sales of similar properties in the area to evaluate the market value of the subject property.

salesperson — a natural person who is employed by a licensed real estate broker to perform acts that require having a real estate license.

salvage value — residual value.

sandwich lease — a leasehold interest that lies between a primary lease and a sublease.

sash — frames that contain one or more windowpanes.

scarcity — a lack of abundance.

scrap value — residual value.

second mortgage — a security instrument that holds second-priority claim against certain property identified in the instrument.

secondary financing — second mortgage and junior mortgage property financing

secondary mortgage market — the market where mortgages are sold by primary mortgage lenders to investors.

secret profit — any compensation or beneficial gain realized by an agent not disclosed to the principal. Real estate agents must always disclose any interest that they or their relatives have in a transaction and obtain their principals' consent.

section — one square mile, containing 640 acres.

sections and township land description — a method of land description based on a grid system of north-south lines ("ranges") and east-west lines ("tier" or "township" lines) that divides the land into townships and sections.

security instrument — the written instrument by which a debtor pledges property as collateral to secure a loan.

SEER — (see EER)

Self-Contained Report — a type of appraisal report that contains a complete description of the data relied on, including data about the neighborhood as well as the property; the reasons the appraiser used for his or her interpretation of the estimate of value; and pertinent maps, photographs, charts, and the plot plans.

self-help eviction — a landlord's denial of possession of leased premises to a tenant without complying with the legal process of eviction.

seller carry back loan — a loan or credit given by a seller of real property to the purchaser of that property.

Seller Financing Disclosure Law — a California law that requires the seller of real property who carries back a loan to give the purchaser loan disclosures similar to the disclosures required in conventional loans.

seller's agent — a real estate broker appointed by the seller to represent the seller.

selling agent — the real estate agent who sells or finds and obtains a buyer for the property in a real estate transaction.

senior mortgage — a mortgage that, relative to another mortgage, has a higher lien-priority position.

separate property — property that is owned in severalty by a spouse or registered domestic partner. Separate property includes property acquired before marriage or the registering of domestic partnership, and property acquired as a gift or by inheritance during marriage or registered domestic partnership.

servient tenement — land that is burdened by an easement.

settlement — *see*, closing

severalty — ownership of property by one person.

sheriff's deed — a deed given at the foreclosure of a property, subsequent to a judgment for foreclosure of a money judgment against the owner or of a mortgage against the property. A sheriff's deed contains no warranties and transfers only the former owner's interest in the property.

sheriff's sale — a sale of property following a judicial foreclosure.

Sherman Act — the federal law passed in 1890 that prohibits agreements, verbal or written, that have the effect of restraining free trade.

short sale — a pre-foreclosure sale made by the borrower (usually with the help of a real estate agent) with lender approval of real estate for less than the balance due on the mortgage loan.

short-term capital gain — the capital gain on the sale of a capital asset that was held for a relatively short period of time, usually one year or less.

sill — the board or metal forming the lower side of the frame for a window or door; the lowest part of the frame of a house, resting on the foundation and providing the base for the studs.

simple interest — the type of interest that is generated only on the principal invested.

single agency — an agency in which a broker represents either the seller or the buyer, but not both.

single point of contact — an individual or team of personnel employed by a mortgage loan servicer, each of whom has the ability and authority to assist a borrower in assessing whether the borrower may be able to take advantage of a foreclosure prevention alternative offered by, or through, the mortgage servicer.

special agent — an agent for a particular act or transaction.

specific lien — a lien that attaches only to specific property.

specific performance — a court order that requires a person to perform according to the terms of a contract.

spot zoning — an improper use of zoning whereby a particular property is zoned differently from similar property similarly situated in the neighborhood.

standard subdivision — is a subdivision with no common areas of ownership or use among the owners of the subdivision parcels.

standby loan commitment — a commitment by a lender to make a take-out loan after construction on a property is completed

State Housing Law — a California state law that provides for minimum construction and occupancy requirements for housing.

statute of frauds — a law that requires certain types of contracts, including most real estate contracts, to be in writing and signed by the party to be bound in order for the contract to be enforceable.

statute of limitations — a law that requires particular types of lawsuits to be brought within a specified time after the occurrence of the event giving rise to the lawsuit.

statutory will — a pre-printed "fill-in-the-blanks" will provided by statute that must be signed in the presence of two competent witnesses.

statutory year — contrasted with a calendar year, a "year" period consisting of 360 days, with 12 months of 30 days (also referred to as a banker's year).

steering — the illegal practice of directing people of protected classes away from, or toward, housing in particular areas.

step-up lease — a graduated lease

stigmatized property — a property having a condition that certain persons may find materially negative in a way that does not relate to the property's actual physical condition.

stock cooperative — a corporation formed or availed of primarily for the purpose of holding title to improved real property either in fee simple or for a term of years.

straight note — a promissory note under which periodic payments consist of interest only.

straight-line depreciation — the expensing of a property by equal amounts over the useful life of the property, determined by subtracting from the cost of the property the estimated residual value of the property and dividing that amount by the useful life of the property measured in years.

straight-line method — a method of calculating annual depreciation of an improvement by dividing the cost of the improvement by the estimated useful life of a typical such improvement.

Street Improvement Act of 1911 — this act provides local governments with the authority to issue bonds to improve streets and make other improvements to specific areas. Assessments on properties are due in equal installments during the term of the bonds, which can run for decades.

studs — vertical wood or metal members in wall or partition framing that serve as the main support for upper floors or roof. Studs are usually placed 16 to 24 inches apart.

subagent — an agent of an agent.

Subdivided Lands Law — a California state law that requires subdividers to disclose certain pertinent information to the initial purchasers of parcels in subdivisions.

Subdivision Map Act — a California state law that gives local officials the authority to regulate subdivisions to ensure that they conform to local general plans.

subjacent support — the support that soil receives from land beneath it.

subject to — acquiring real property that is burdened by a mortgage without becoming personally liable for the mortgage debt.

subjective value — (also referred to as *value in use*) is value placed on the amenities of a property by a specific person.

sublease — a transfer of a tenant's right to a portion of the leased premises or to the entire premises for less than the entire remaining lease term.

subordination clause — a provision in a mortgage or deed of trust that states that the mortgage or deed of trust will have lower priority than a mortgage or deed of trust recorded later.

Summary Report — a type of appraisal report that typically consists of several pages of forms to be filled out by an appraiser that contain pertinent data about the subject property, along with photos, maps, and plans. This type of appraisal report is most often used by lending institutions, insurance companies, and government agencies.

supplemental tax assessment — an event that occurs upon the sale of real property or completion of new construction on real property when the county assessor determines the current market value of the transferred property or the newly constructed real property and subtracts the prior assessed value from the current assessed value to obtain the net supplemental value that will be enrolled as a supplemental assessment. The increase (or decrease) in assessed value is then reflected in a prorated supplemental tax bill that covers the period from the first day of the month following the transfer or completion of construction to the end of the fiscal year, which runs from July 1 to June 30.

take-out loan — a loan that provides long-term financing for a property on which a construction loan had been made.

tax assessor — the county or city official who is responsible for appraising property.

tax auditor — the county or city official who maintains the county tax rolls.

tax collector — the county or city official who is responsible for collecting taxes.

tax deed — the deed given to the successful buyer at a tax sale. A tax deed conveys title free and clear from private liens, but not from certain tax liens or special assessment liens, or from easements and recorded restrictions.

tenancy in common — a form of joint ownership that is presumed to exist if the persons who own the property are neither married nor registered domestic partners and they own undivided interests in property. Tenants in common may hold unequal interests; however, if the deed does not specify fractional interests among the tenants, the interests will be presumed to be equal.

tenancy in partnership — a form of joint ownership in which the partners combine their assets and efforts in a business venture.

tentative map — a map required pursuant to the Subdivision Map Act for subdivisions that create five or more parcels, five or more condominiums, a community apartment project containing 5 or more interests, or the conversion of a dwelling into a stock cooperative of 5 or more dwelling units. The tentative map, which is to be filed with the local planning commission, must include a legal description of the property; the location and description of all adjoining highways, streets, and waterways; the location and description of easements for roads, drainage, sewers, and other public utilities; proposed public areas; and proposed provisions for floods and other natural hazards.

testament — a will.

testator — one who dies leaving a will.

time-share estate — an estate in real property coupled with the right of occupancy for certain periods of time.

time-share use — a right to occupancy during certain periods of time, not coupled to an estate in real property.

title plant — a duplicate of county title records maintained at title insurance companies for use in title searches.

township — six square miles, containing 36 sections.

trade fixtures — objects that a tenant attaches to real property for use in the tenant's trade or business. Trade fixtures differ from other fixtures in that, even though they are attached with some permanence to real property, they may be removed at the end of the tenancy of the business.

transferability — the ability to transfer some interest in property to another.

Treaty of Guadalupe Hidalgo —the treaty that ended the Mexican-American war (1846-48), annexed California to the United States, and provided for the recognition of community property rights in California.

triggering term — any of a number of specific finance terms stated in an advertisement for a loan that triggers Regulation Z disclosure requirements in the advertisement.

triple net lease — a lease under which the tenant pays a fixed rent plus the landlord's property taxes, hazard insurance, and all maintenance costs.

trust deed — a three-party security device, the three parties being the borrower (*trustor*), the lender (*beneficiary*), and a third-party (*trustee)* to whom "bare legal title" is conveyed.

trust fund overage — a situation in which a trust fund account balance is greater than it should be.

trust fund shortage — a situation in which a trust fund account balance is less than it should be.

trustee — a person who holds something of value in trust for the benefit of another; under a deed of trust, a neutral third-party who holds naked legal title for security.

trustor — a borrower who executes a deed of trust.

Truth-in-Lending Act (TILA) — a federal consumer protection law that was enacted in 1968 with the intention of helping borrowers understand the costs of borrowing money by requiring disclosures about loan terms and costs (in particular, the APR) and to standardize the way in which certain costs related to the loan are calculated and disclosed.

tying arrangement — occurs in antitrust law when the seller conditions the sale of one product or service on the purchase of another product or service.

underwriter — one who analyzes the risk of, and recommends whether to approve, a proposed mortgage loan.

undivided interest — an ownership interest in property in which an owner has the right of possession of the entire property and may not exclude the other owners from any portion by claiming that a specific portion of the property is his or hers alone.

undivided interest subdivision — a subdivision in which owners own a partial or fractional interest in an entire parcel of land. The land in an undivided interest subdivision is not divided; its ownership is divided.

unenforceable contract — a contract that a court would not enforce.

Uniform Commercial Code (UCC) — a set of laws that established unified and comprehensive regulations for security transactions of personal property and that superseded existing laws in that field.

unilateral contract — a contract in which one party gives a promise that is to be accepted not by another promise but by performance.

unity of interest — in reference to joint ownership, refers to each of the owners having equal interests in the property.

unity of possession — in reference to joint ownership, refers to each of the owners having an equal, undivided right to possession of the entire property.

unity of time — in reference to joint ownership, refers to each of the owners having acquired his/her interest in the property at the same time.

unity of title — in reference to joint ownership, refers to each of the owners having received ownership in the property from the same deed.

unlawful detainer — a legal action to regain possession of real property.

Unruh Civil Rights Act — a California state law that prohibits persons engaged in business from discriminating on the basis of race, color, religion, ancestry, national origin, gender, disability, medical condition, or age when providing products or services in California. In housing related activities, businesses are also prohibited from discriminating on the basis of marital status, familial status, sexual orientation, or source of income. This law applies to all real estate salespersons and brokers.

useful life — the estimated period during which a property generates revenue (if the property is an income property) or usefulness (if the property, such as a private residence, has value other than income value).

usury — the charging of interest in excess of that allowed by law.

utility — the usefulness of property; its ability to satisfy a potential buyer's need or desire, such as to provide shelter or income.

VA — the Department of Veterans Affairs is a federal agency designed to benefit veterans and members of their families.

Vacation Ownership and Time-Share Act of 2004 — a California state consumer protection law that regulates disclosures and representations made by time-share salespersons.

valid contract — a contract that is binding and enforceable in a court of law.

value — the present worth of all rights to future benefits, arising out of property ownership, to typical users or investors.

variance — an exception that may be granted in cases where damage to the value of a property from the strict enforcement of zoning ordinances would far outweigh any benefit to be derived from enforcement.

vendee — the purchaser in a real property sales agreement

vendor — the seller in a real property sales agreement.

veteran's exemption — and exemption of up to $4,000 from the assessed value of a qualified veteran's property.

vicarious liability — liability imposed on a person not because of that person's own acts but because of the acts of another. (See, respondeat superior.)

void contract — a purported contract that has no legal effect.

voidable contract — a contract that, at the request of one party only, may be declared unenforceable, but is valid until it is so declared.

voluntary lien — a lien obtained through the voluntary action of the one against whose property the lien attaches.

Vrooman Street Act of 1885 — this act provides local governments with authority to construct streets, sewers, and other improvements. Funds for these improvements are secured by the issuance of bonds, which are redeemed by assessing the properties benefited.

warranty deed — a deed in which the grantor warrants that the title being conveyed is good and free from defects or encumbrances, and that the grantor will defend the title against all suits.

warranty of habitability — mandated by both statutes and by common law, an implied warranty in any residential lease that the premises are suitable for human habitation.

will — a document that stipulates how one's property should be distributed after death; also called a testament.

writ — a court order commanding the person to whom it is directed to perform an act specified therein.

writ of attachment — a writ ordering the seizure of property belonging to a defendant to ensure the availability of the property to satisfy a judgment if the plaintiff wins.

writ of execution — a writ directing a public official (usually the sheriff) to seize and sell property of a debtor to satisfy a debt.

writ of possession — a court order that authorizes the sheriff or other eviction authority to remove a tenant and the tenant's possessions from leased premises.

zoning — laws of a city or county that specify the type of land-use that is acceptable in certain areas.

Math Review for Real Estate

It is best while studying this math review and working through the questions presented to have a basic calculator handy (one that simply adds, subtracts, multiplies and divides — not a "scientific" or a "financial" calculator). Currently, the centers where real estate license exams are given supply a basic calculator to each examinee (you are not permitted to bring your own), so getting used to solving math problems on such a calculator is highly recommended.

There is no indication from past exams that you need to be familiar with math concepts beyond what is taught in grade school, so even if math was never your favorite subject, you should not fear the types of questions that appear on real estate license exams. Remember, you will be taking an exam on real estate principles, not a math exam. The only math you are expected to know is the basic math that will help you solve practical, everyday real estate problems like the problems presented here. Memorize the few measurement correspondences below, become familiar with a few simple equations and how they apply to practical real estate problems, and you'll do just fine.

Here are the measurement correspondences that you should memorize:

- 1 mile = 5,280 feet or 320 rods
- 1 rod = 16½ ft.
- 1 township = 6 mi. x 6 mi. = 36 sections
- 1 section = 1 mi. x 1 mi. = 640 acres
- 1 acre = 43,560 square feet
- 1 square acre ≈ 208.7 ft. x 208.7 ft. (i.e., a "square acre" has 208.7 ft. on each side.)

Also, remember that a *commercial acre* = the buildable part of an acre that remains after subtracting land needed for streets, sidewalks, alleys, curbs, etc.

CONVERTING DECIMALS, PERCENTAGES, AND FRACTIONS

To convert a percentage to a decimal, simply remove the % sign and move the decimal point two places to the left:

15% → .15

74.6% → .746

To convert a decimal to a percent, move the decimal point two places to the right and add the % sign:

.75 → 75%

1.12 → 112%

To convert a fraction to a decimal, divide the numerator (the number on top) by the denominator (the number on the bottom):

1/5 → 1÷5 → .20

3/4 → 3÷4 → .75

Many everyday real estate issues involve percentages: commissions, rate of return on investments, depreciation, and proration. We will discuss examples of each of these kinds of issues and how percentages apply to each.

Commission Problems:

Because nearly every real estate agent expects to receive commissions (many, hopefully!), it is not unlikely that a question or two relating to commissions might appear on an exam.

Example 1: *Jessica is a real estate salesperson who found a buyer for a home that sold for $800,000. Jessica's employing broker received a 5% commission for the sale. The agreement between the broker and Jessica provides that she receive 40% of the broker's commission on every sale she procures. What is Jessica's commission on this transaction?*

Here the solution is to first find the broker's commission:

5% of $800,000 = .05 x $800,000 = $40,000. Jessica is to receive 40% of $40,000 = .40 x $40,000 = $16,000.

Another way to think about such a problem is to note that Jessica receives 40% of 5% = .40 x .05 = .02 = 2% of the sales price. Using this 2% figure, we find that 2% of $800,000 = .02 x 800,000 = $16,000.

Example 2: A somewhat more interesting problem (writers of textbooks are fond of using the word "interesting" rather than "difficult") is as follows:

Bob is a salesperson who works for broker Janet. Bob's agreement with Janet is that he gets a commission of 40% of whatever commission Janet receives on sales made by Bob. Bob procures a sale of a house that was listed by broker Susan, who had a cooperating agent agreement with Janet to split the commission on the sale 50-50. Susan's listing agreement with the owner called for a 6% commission. Bob's commission on the sale was $6,000. How much did the house sell for?

Because they tend to be long-winded, these types of problems *appear* to involve much more thought than they actually do — they simply need to be approached methodically, step-by-simple-step, until the answer falls out:

The problem tells us that:

$6,000 = 40% of 50% of 6% of Sales Price

$$= (.4 \times .5 \times .06) \times \text{Sales Price}$$

$$= .012 \times \text{Sales Price (i.e., 1.2\% of Sales Price)}$$

Therefore, dividing each side of the equation by .012, we get

$500,000 = Sales Price

Example 3: *Ernesto sold his house, receiving for $423,000 after paying a 6% commission. For how much did Ernesto sell his house?*

We are told that the price the house sold for — its "Sales Price" — minus the commission paid was $423,000. Therefore,

Sales Price - Commission = $423,000

Sales Price - (6% of Sales Price) = $423,000

Sales price - (.06 × Sales Price) = $423,000

.94 × Sales Price = $423,000

Finally, dividing both sides of the equation by .94, we get

Sales Price = $450,000

Investment Problems:

Investment problems involve four concepts:

1. Investment — the amount of dollars invested
2. Income — the amount of dollars earned (or lost) from the investment
3. Rate — the rate of return on the investment (often referred to as the "ROI")
4. Time — the amount of time the Investment is earning the Rate

Investment problems involve the following relationships (formula):

Income = Investment x Rate x Time Income

When dealing with investment problems (as well as with other problems, such as profit and loss, interest, and depreciation problems), it is ***crucially important*** to carefully pay close attention to the time periods provided, and asked for, in the question. If there are different time periods presented, the first thing you should do is convert all the periods to the same value measured in years, quarters, months or days.

Example 4: *Joe wants to make $750 per month from an investment that will earn 5% per year. How much must Joe invest to obtain his desired monthly investment income?*

Here we are told that Joe wants to earn $750 *per month*, which is

12 x $750 = $9,000 *per year*. Therefore, the problem has given us

Income = $9,000 (per year)

Rate = 5% (per year)

Putting these given bits of information into our formula, we have:

$9,000 = 5% (*per year*) of Investment for 1 year

= .05 (per year) x Investment x 1 year

By dividing both sides of this equation by .05, we get

$9,000 ÷ .05 = Investment

$180,000 = Investment

The question in Example 4 involved the rate of return on Joe's investment where the investment Joe made (the principal) was not yet converted back into dollars. Such a situation usually involves investing money in some kind of interest-bearing account. Other investment problems involve situations where the principal amount invested (the Investment) is eventually sold (the Sales Price). In such problems Income = Sales Price - Investment.

Therefore, the investment formula

Income = Investment x Rate x Time

becomes:

Sales Price – Investment = Investment x Rate x Time

Example 5: *Sarah bought her house for $300,000 and sold it for $375,000 five years later. What was the rate of return on her investment?*

The problem tells us that Sarah's Income (Sales Price - Investment) is $75,000. Therefore,

$75,000 = Investment x Rate (*per year*) x Time (in *years*)

$75,000 = $300,000 x Rate (*per year*) x 5 (*years*)

[Remember to keep the time periods consistent throughout the formula!]

Therefore, by dividing both sides of the equation by

$300,000 x 5 (years) we get:

$75,000 ÷ ($300,000 x 5 years) = Rate (per year)

.05 (per year) = Rate (per year)

5% (per year) = Rate (per year)

Note that if the question asked for the rate per month, the answer would be .05/12 = .00417 (rounded off) or .417% per month.

Investors in property are often concerned with what is called the **capitalization rate** (the "cap rate"), which is simply what we have been calling Rate calculated on an annual basis and where the Income is the net annual income of the property.

Example 6: *Susan is interested in a building that she has learned produces $100,000 net income per year. The capitalization rate that she wants to earn is 8%. What is the maximum price she should pay for this building?*

The maximum price she should pay would be the amount of Investment that would yield Income of $100,000 each year at the Rate of 8% per year. Using our formula

Income = Investment x Rate x Time, we get

$100,000 = Investment x 8% x 1 year

$100,000 = Investment x .08

$1,250,000 = Investment

Investors also sometimes purchase promissory notes at a discount, as in the following example:

Example 7: *Susan owns a promissory note for $10,000 payable in 12 months at a rate of 6% interest, which is also payable at the end of the note term. Wanting to convert the note into cash, Susan sells the note to her friend Bob at a 5% discount. Assuming that the note and interest are paid in full at the end of the note term, what rate of return will Bob receive?*

Here the question asks for a Rate, so we must figure out the amount of Income Bob will earn and the amount of his Investment. His Investment is $10,000 - (5% of $10,000) = $10,000 - $500 = $9,500. His income is 6% of

$10,000 + $500 which is $600 + $500 = $1,100. Therefore, Bob's Rate = Income ÷ Investment which is $1,100 ÷ $9,500 = 11.58% (rounded off).

Depreciation Problems:

Although many different ways to calculate depreciation are allowed by law (depending on what law one has to satisfy), the only method of depreciation that appears to be tested on real estate license exams is **straight-line depreciation**, which assumes that the property depreciates by an *equal amount* each year.

Depreciation is based on what is considered the **useful life** (also referred to as the **economic life**) of the property and on the estimated **residual value** (also referred to as **salvage value** or **scrap value**) of the property at the end of the property's useful life. Some things, such as computers, have a much shorter useful life than do buildings, so it is always important when considering depreciation to know what the useful life of the item being depreciated is. The straight-line depreciation is defined as:

$$Annual\ Depreciation = \frac{Cost\ of\ Property\ -\ Residual\ Value}{useful\ life\ of\ the\ property\ in\ years}$$

Thus, if the property has a 5-year useful life and no residual value, the rate of (straight-line) depreciation is:

$$\frac{100\%}{5\ years} = 20\%\ per\ year$$

Example 8: *Evan purchases a building for $3,000,000 that has a useful life of 30 years and salvage value of $0. After 10 years, what is the value of the building, if by "value" we mean the original cost less accumulated straight-line depreciation?*

Here the depreciation rate is:

$$\frac{100\%}{30\ years} = 3\ 1/3\ \%\ per\ year$$

$$3\ ^1/_3\%\ per\ year \times 10\ years = 33\ 1/3\%\ depreciation$$

33 1/3% of the initial value $= 33\ 1/3\% \times \$3\ million\ = \$1,000,000$

Therefore, value = cost - depreciation = $2,000,000

Interest Problems: Interest is the "rent" we pay to possess, use, and enjoy someone else's money. The yearly rent for each dollar we use (borrow) is called the interest rate — if we pay 8¢ each year for each dollar, the interest rate is 8% per year.

Interest problems generally involve four simple concepts:

1.   *Interest Rate* (which, to avoid wordiness, we will call Rate);
2.   *Principal* (the amount of money borrowed);
3.   *Time* (the number of years or fraction of years the principal is borrowed);
4.   *Interest Due and Owing* (which we will call Interest).

Because the interest due and owing (Interest) is equal to the interest rate (Rate) times the amount of money borrowed (Principal) times the amount of time the money is borrowed (Time),

Interest = Rate x Principal x Time

The above formula is known as **simple interest**, which considers interest to be generated only on the principal invested. A more rapid method of generating interest earnings is referred to as compounding. **Compound interest** is generated when accumulated interest is reinvested to generate interest earnings from previous interest earnings. Though the amount of interest generated can be revved up by compounding yearly, semiannually, quarterly, daily, or even continuously, real estate exams stick with simple interest, as do most real estate loans on which interest is paid monthly. There is a story — perhaps apocryphal — that Albert Einstein once said that the power of compounding is the eighth wonder of the world.

When calculating interest, it is also important to know what **day count convention** to use. An exact interest calculation would take into account the precise number of days money is loaned: 30 days for some months, 31 or 28 or 29 for other months; 365 days for some years, 366 for leap years. In the days before computers, such calculations would have been quite burdensome, so the **30/360 day count convention** was adopted to simplify interest calculations. When using the 30/360 day count convention, each month is considered to have 30 days, and each year is considered to have 360 days. A year consisting of 360 days with 12 months of 30 days each is often referred to as a **statutory year**, or a banker's year. The 30/360 day count convention for calculating interest is standard in the real estate market, is the method used on real estate exams, and is the method that will be used throughout this text. Interest calculated by the 30/360 day count convention is referred to as **ordinary interest**.

Example 9: *What is the interest on a $400,000 loan for 1 year, 2 months, and 10 days at 6% interest (using a statutory year)?*

The time elapsed is 360 days + 60 days + 10 days = 430 days.

430 ÷ 360 = 1.19444 years. Therefore, applying our formula

Interest = Rate x Principal x Time, we get

Interest = .06 x $400,000 x 1.19444 = $28,666.56

Example 10: *Jessica borrows $12,000 from her friend Susan. The terms of the loan are that principal will be paid back in equal monthly installments over a five-year period along with the interest that was generated at the annual rate of 6% during the month on the outstanding balance of principal owing. What is Jessica's payment to Susan at the end of the second month?*

To answer this question, we first have to answer another question; namely, how much principal does Jessica pay Susan at the end of the first month? This is due to the fact that Susan's first month payment will reduce the principal amount on which the second month payment must be calculated.

Because there are 60 months in 5 years, the amount of Susan's monthly payment attributable to principal is $12,000 ÷ 60 = $200. Therefore, the amount of principal owed after the first-month payment is made is $12,000 - $200 = $11,800. Consequently, the second-month payment will be $200 + the interest due on $11,800 *for one month*. Because the interest rate is 6% annually, the monthly rate is 1/2%. Thus, the second month payment is $200 + 1/2% of $11,800 = $259.

Amortization Charts

Although interest and principal payments for loans are now calculated on financial calculators or on calculation software freely available on the Internet, we will look briefly at a simplified amortization chart to get a feel for how such a chart was used (in the old days) to calculate the monthly payments for fixed-rate loans at various interest rates. (See figure below).

The chart displays in the left column the interest rate, and in columns to the right, the term in years of a fixed-rate, fully amortized loan. To find the monthly payment *per $1,000* principal borrowed, simply find the intersection of the rate and term of the loan.

Monthly Payment Per $1,000 on Fixed-Rate, Fully Amortized Loans				
Rate	10-year term	15-year term	30-year term	40-year term
4%	10.125	7.397	4.775	4.180
5%	10.607	7.908	5.369	4.822
6%	11.102	8.439	5.996	5.503
7%	11.611	8.989	6.653	6.215
8%	12.133	9.557	7.338	6.954

Example 11: *Susan makes payments of $936 per month, including 6% interest on a fixed-rate, fully amortized 30-year loan. What was the initial amount of her loan?*

Finding where 6% and a 30-year term intersect in the chart, we obtain the number 5.996 which is the dollar amount per month per $1,000 of initial loan.

$936 ÷ 5.996 = $156.104 per $1,000.

$156.104 x 1000 = $156,104

Proration Problems:

As a general rule, at the close of escrow in a real estate transaction certain allocations of expenses incurred in the ordinary course of property ownership must be made. For example, if the escrow closes midyear or midmonth, the seller may have prepaid taxes, insurance, or association dues, in which case credit to the seller's account should be made. Conversely, if the seller is behind on paying taxes or insurance, etc., the seller's account should be debited. Such an adjustment of expenses that either have been paid or are in arrears in proportion to actual time of ownership as of the closing or other agreed-upon date is called **proration**. Proration, like ordinary interest, is generally calculated according to the 30/360 day count convention (statutory year).

To compute proration, follow these steps:

1. determine which, if any, expenses are to be prorated;
2. determine to whom the expenses should be credited or debited;
3. determine how many days the expenses are to be prorated;
4. calculate the per day proration amount; and
5. multiply the number of days by the per day proration amount.

Example 12: *Susan purchased a condo that had been rented from Bob at $1,500 a month. Escrow closed on September 16. Who pays whom in regard to proration of the rent?*

Rent is normally collected *in advance* on the first day of the month, so unless stated otherwise one should make this assumption in proration of rent problems. Under this assumption, Bob received $1,500 on or about September 1, but only deserved to keep half of the month's rent because Susan acquired ownership of the condo on September 16. Therefore, Susan should be credited $750 at the close of escrow.

Example 13: *Emily purchased a home from Bob on which Bob had an outstanding loan balance of $385,000 on April 20, the day that escrow closed. The interest rate on the loan was 5% and was payable with the loan payment on the first of each month. If Emily assumed Bob's loan, who should have paid whom in regard to proration of the interest?*

Interest on home loans is normally paid *after* it has accrued, and we will make that assumption here. Therefore, the seller, Bob, owned the home for 19 days before closing — 19 days for which he had not paid the interest on the loan as of the closing of escrow. Emily should, therefore, have been credited for 19 day's interest.

The annual interest on the loan was 5%, and $385,000 was the loan balance on which interest would be paid by Emily (who assumed the loan) on May 1. Figured on an *annual* basis, interest of 5% on $385,000 = $19,250, so to obtain the *daily* interest amount for each day of April we divide $19,250 by 360 (using a statutory year) to get $53.4722. [Note that in proration problems it is best to use at least four numbers after the decimal point until you get to the final answer, which can be rounded off.] Because Emily should have been credited for 19 days, her credit should have been 19 x $53.4722 = $1,015.97.

Length and Square Footage Problems

When calculating the square footage of something, remember that the area of a rectangle is base x height and the area of a triangle is ½ x base x height.

<u>Example 14</u>: *Kevin is going to purchase the lot shown in the diagram below and build on it a house and garage, also shown in the diagram below. He has been quoted the following:*

- *$150 per square foot for the house*
- *$40 per square foot for the garage*
- *$10 per square foot for the land*

What is the total amount that Evan will pay for this lot, house, and garage?

First we calculate the square footage of each item:

house area = 60' x 30' = 1,800 ft.²

garage area = 25' x 18' = 450 ft.²

lot area = ½ x 100 x 150 = 7,500 ft.²

cost of house = 1800 ft.² x $150 per ft.² = $270,000

cost of garage = 450 ft.² x $40 per ft.² = $18,000

cost of the lot = 7500 ft.² x $10 per ft.² = $75,000

Total = $363,000

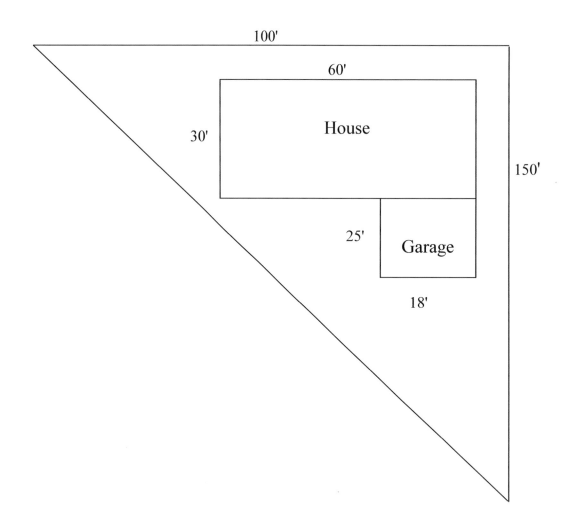

Practice Exam #1:

1. If with lender approval a California homeowner sells his or her home for less than the balance due on a mortgage secured by the home
   a. the lender may collect no deficiency on the short sale
   b. neither the IRS nor the Franchise Tax Board will treat as income the short-sale debt cancellation
   c. both a and b
   d. neither a nor b

2. Solid minerals that lie beneath a parcel of land that is transferred
   a. pass with the deed
   b. pass with the deed unless specifically excluded
   c. do not pass with the deed because they are owned by the state until captured
   d. are subject to the law of capture

3. A nonprofit company created to provide water supplies for property owners in a specific district is called a
   a. subdivided land corporation
   b. township utility
   c. leaseback water company
   d. mutual water company

4. An easement that encumbers a servient tenement might be
   a. an easement appurtenant
   b. an easement in gross
   c. either a or b
   d. neither a nor b

5. In regard to the creation of easements, which of the following terms least belongs with the others?
   a. prescription
   b. encumbrance
   c. necessity
   d. express grant

6. A property described as the W 1/2 of the NW 1/4, the SE 1/4 of the N 1/2, and the SE 1/4 of the SE 1/4 of the E 1/2 of Section 3 contains how many acres?

    a. 160
    b. 180
    c. 200
    d. none of the above

7. The right of a cable company to lay cable under a person's land is

    a. an appurtenant easement
    b. a nuisance in gross
    c. a subterranean right
    d. an easement in gross

8. A condition subsequent would likely be enforced by the

    a. local zoning commission
    b. local district attorney
    c. grantor
    d. local sheriff

9. A branch of a tree on Bob's property extends over Jane's property. Jane

    a. may cut down the tree
    b. must simply put up with this minor nuisance
    c. may cut and remove the branch up to the property line
    d. both a and c

10. The transfer of real property is completed by the delivery of

    a. a deed
    b. a bill of sale
    c. a mortgage
    d. an appurtenance

11. If at the end of a life estate, the future interest arises in someone other than the grantor, the residue of the estate is called a

    a. less-than-freehold estate

b. reversion

c. condition subsequent

d. remainder

12. A condition subsequent would most likely be

a. found in a deed

b. a reversion

c. a remainder

d. a license to use

13. A lease for one month would be

a. an estate at sufferance

b. an estate for years

c. an estate at will

d. periodic tenancy

14. A grants to B a life estate for the life of C. If B dies before C

a. C acquires an estate for the term of C's life

b. the estate reverts to A

c. the estate passes to B's heirs or devisees

d. C acquires an estate for the term of A's life

15. The four types of leasehold estates differ according to their

a. creation

b. duration

c. both a and b

d. neither a nor b

16. The type of lease that lasts for specific period of time is called a

a. tenancy at will

b. periodic tenancy

c. tenancy for years

d. none of the above

17. The characteristic(s) of a tenancy for years include

a. continues for a definite term

b. the term may not exceed 49 years

c. has specific beginning and ending dates

d. both a and c

18. A lease for 33 days would describe
   a. periodic tenancy
   b. estate for years
   c. estate at will
   d. estate at sufferance

19. An estate at will can be terminated
   a. without notice
   b. only after a court orders eviction
   c. by either party at any time
   d. none of the above

20. A lease in real estate conveys to the tenant
   a. a nonexclusive right to possess
   b. an exclusive right to possess
   c. an irrevocable remainder
   d. a license

21. If an intestate decedent is survived by a domestic partner and two children, how much of the decedent's separate property does each child received?
   a. 1/2
   b. 1/3
   c. 1/4
   d. 1/6

22. If the highest initial bid for a property at a probate sale was $90,000, any late bid must be for at least
   a. $91,000
   b. $92,000
   c. $95,000
   d. $94,000

23. Which of the following is (are) false?

a. avulsion is addition to land acquired by the gradual accumulation of soil through the action of water

b. alluvium is a process that occurs when a river or stream suddenly carries away a part of a bank and deposits it downstream, either on the same or opposite bank

c. both a and b

d. neither a nor b

24. In the case of avulsion, how long does the owner of the carried-away property have to reclaim his or her property before it becomes part of the property onto which it settled?

a. 2 years

b. 1 year

c. 6 months

d. once the carried-away property is deposited, it automatically becomes part of the property onto which it settled.

25. Which of the following terms least belongs with the others?

a. abandonment

b. accretion

c. adverse possession

d. prescription

26. For a grant deed to be valid, it must be

a. acknowledged

b. recorded

c. delivered

d. all of the above

27. Which of the following terms least belongs with the others?

a. eminent domain

b. police power

c. taking for public use

d. just compensation

28. A valid deed must

a. be dated

b. be recorded

c. be signed by a competent grantee

d. none of the above

29. Eminent domain is similar to
   a. public grant
   b. condemnation
   c. escheat
   d. adverse possession

30. A person who dies intestate dies
   a. without heirs
   b. without leaving a will
   c. leaving a will
   d. both a and c

31. A transfers his property to his sister, B, and to a corporation, C, in which he is a shareholder, "as joint tenants."
   a. B and C are joint tenants
   b. B and C are tenants in common
   c. B and C are tenants in partnership
   d. B and C are tenants at will

32. A and B own property as joint tenants. Their joint tenancy may be terminated
   a. through a voluntary partition
   b. through judicial determination after a filing of a partition action
   c. either a or b
   d. neither a nor b

33. Which of the following is (are) false?
   a. tenants in common may not commit waste against the property
   b. tenants in common have an undivided interest in the property
   c. both a and b
   d. neither a nor b

34. A and B own a property as joint tenants. B wills her interest in the property to C and subsequently dies.
   a. C receives B's interest as an heir
   b. C receives B's interest as a devisee
   c. C and A are tenants in common
   d. none of the above

35. Regarding community property,
   a. there is only one title to the property
   b. each spouse or registered domestic partner owns one-half interest in the property
   c. both a and b
   d. neither a nor b

36. Jane and Bob are married. Bob may dispose by will
   a. a joint tenancy interest
   b. a tenancy in common interest that is not part of community property
   c. all of the community property
   d. both b and c

37. Sisters Jane and Susan inherit property from their parents. They might own the property as
   a. joint tenants
   b. tenants in common
   c. community property
   d. either a or b

38. The most important characteristic of joint tenancy is
   a. unity of time
   b. right of survivorship
   c. equal right to possession
   d. equal right to convey

39. Joint tenants have all of the following except
   a. right of survivorship
   b. right to will good title to another

c. equal right of possession

d. right to sell their interest to another

40. While she was single, Jane owned a condo. After Jane and Bob marry and move into the condo, the condo is held as

a. community property

b. joint tenancy

c. separate property, unless otherwise agreed

d. community property with right of survivorship

41. Which of the following is (are) false?

a. a notice of pendency of action is a lien

b. a lis pendens serves as constructive notice to prospective purchasers of a property that a lawsuit affecting title to the property is pending

c. both a and b

d. neither a nor b

42. An attachment lien

a. cannot be foreclosed on if not paid

b. is also referred to as a lis pendens

c. is a voluntary lien

d. is a writ authorizing the seizure of property

43. To obtain an attachment lien, the amount in controversy must be

a. $10,000 or more

b. $1,000 or more

c. $500 or more

d. $1,500 or more

44. Which of the following are specific liens?

a. real property tax liens

b. judgment liens

c. both a and b

d. neither a nor b

45. Which of the following is (are) false?

a. a preliminary notice must be given within 10 days after first providing labor or materials for work of improvement

b. an unlicensed contractor may not apply for mechanics lien

74

c. both a and b

d. neither a nor b

46. Liens placed on real property to enforce the collection of real property taxes are

a. general liens

b. specific liens

c. construction liens

d. homestead liens

47. Which of the following words is least related to the others?

a. mechanics lien

b. lis pendens

c. tax lien

d. preliminary notice

48. Which of the following words is least related to the others?

a. judgment lien

b. abstract of judgment

c. involuntary lien

d. voluntary lien

49. Which of the following documents must be recorded to be valid?

a. declared homestead

b. automatic homestead

c. notice of nonresponsibility

d. both a and c

50. Bob contracts with Joe to have a pergola constructed in the backyard of a house Bob leases from Sally. Sally can protect herself from liability for the construction by posting and recording a

a. notice of nonliability

b. notice of nonresponsibility

c. notice of cessation

d. notice a quitclaim

51. A minor can become emancipated by
   a. becoming validly married
   b. serving in the military
   c. both a and b
   d. neither a nor b

52. Which of the following is (are) false?
   a. mutual consent (often referred to as a "meeting of the minds") is usually evidenced by an offer of one party that manifests contractual intention and by an acceptance by the other party
   b. menace refers to a threat of duress or of injury to person or property of a person
   c. both a and b
   d. neither a nor b

53. Which of the following terms least belongs with the others?
   a. contingency
   b. offer
   c. mutual consent
   d. acceptance

54. A counteroffer
   a. is effective when sent
   b. is a rejection of the original offer
   c. both a and b
   d. neither a nor b

55. An offer can be terminated
   a. by a revocation of the offer
   b. by a rejection of the offer
   c. both a and b
   d. neither a nor b

56. A counteroffer by an offeree
   a. revokes the offeror's offer
   b. presents an offer to the offeror
   c. terminates the offeror's offer

d. both b and c

57. A contract that, at the request of one party only, may be declared unenforceable, but is valid until it is so declared, is called
    a. an executory contract
    b. a void contract
    c. a voidable contract
    d. a unilateral contract

58. In California, the Statute of Limitations for written contracts generally is
    a. 1 year
    b. 2 years
    c. 4 years
    d. 10 years

59. Bob enters into an oral contract with Joe to rent Joe's apartment for 9 months. The contract is
    a. voidable because of the statute of frauds
    b. not void because of the statute of frauds
    c. void because of the statute of frauds
    d. illegal because of the statute of frauds

60. A contract that has been fully performed by all parties is called
    a. executory
    b. voidable
    c. unilateral
    d. executed

61. The law that requires the authorization of an agent to be of the same formality as is required for the act(s) the agent is hired to perform is called
    a. the statute of limitations
    b. the equal dignities rule
    c. the rule against negative fraud

d. the law against self-help eviction

62. Agency by implication and ostensible agency differ in that
    a. in ostensible agency the supposed agent is found to owe agency duties to the principal
    b. in agency by implication the agent and the principal are found to be liable for their actions to a third party
    c. neither a nor b
    d. both a and b

63. Which of the following is (are) false?
    a. state and federal taxing authorities recognize a salesperson as an employee of the broker by requiring the broker to withdraw certain taxes from the salesperson's paycheck
    b. the CalBRE regulates the relationship between the broker and his or her salespersons as employer-employee relationships
    c. neither a nor b
    d. both a and b

64. Which of the following is (are) true?
    a. a third party who is aware that he or she is dealing with an authorized agent has the duty to ascertain the purpose and scope of the agency
    b. though a principal is liable to third parties for the actions of an agent who acts within his or her authority, no liability is incurred by a principal for the acts of an agent beyond the scope of the agent's actual or ostensible authority
    c. both a and b
    d. either a nor b

65. Which of the following is (are) false?
    a. commingling results from the failure to properly segregate the funds belonging to the agent from the funds received and held on behalf of the seller or buyer
    b. commingling is the unauthorized misappropriation and use of another's funds or other property
    c. both a and b
    d. neither a nor b

66. California's antitrust law is based upon the
    a. Cartwright Act
    b. Realty Competition Act

c. Sherman Antitrust Act

d. none of the above

67. Which of the following is not relevant in determining whether a person is an independent contractor?

a. the employer's degree of supervision of the person

b. the number of hours the person works

c. whether the employer provides an office for the person to work in

d. whether the employer withholds Social Security contributions for the person

68. A fiduciary relationship exists between

a. a real estate agent and his or her principal

b. a seller and a buyer

c. a listing agent and a potential buyer

d. both a and c

69. Bob and Sally are brokers who own separate realty companies. Over lunch one day, Sally tells Bob how her sales plan works and encourages Bob to try it out. Bob doesn't respond one way or the other, but the next day he announces to his salespersons that the company will be adopting a new 6% commission sales plan — the one that Sally told him she was using.

a. Sally may be found guilty of price fixing.

b. Bob may be found guilty of price fixing.

c. Both Sally and Bob may be found guilty of price fixing.

d. none of the above

70. Sally reasonably believes that Joe is acting as her agent, and Joe fails to correct her impression.

a. Joe and Sally probably have an agency relationship by implication.

b. Joe and Sally probably have an agency relationship by ratification.

c. Joe and Sally probably have an agency relationship by estoppel.

d. none of the above

71. Emily owns an apartment building worth $4,500,000 on which she earns 9% gross annual income. What is her monthly gross income from this investment?
   a. $33,750
   b. $40,500
   c. $405,000
   d. $36,450

72. Susan is a salesperson who sold a 1/4 acre lot for $17 per square foot. The commission rate her broker received was 8%, and Susan split the commission with her broker 50-50. How much did Susan earn on the sale?
   a. $29,620.80
   b. $14,810.40
   c. $7,405.20
   d. none of the above

73. Emily, Susan, and Janet are partners who own a building that produces rent of $17,000 per month. Susan owns a 41% interest in the building. How much rental income from the building does Susan earn each year?
   a. $6,970
   b. $68,000
   c. $8,500
   d. none of the above

74. Jon financed his home with an 85% loan at a fixed annual rate of 5½%. Jon paid $3,895.83 interest the first month. How much did Jon pay for the house (rounded to the nearest dollar)?
   a. $849,999
   b. $722,499
   c. $70,833
   d. $999,999

75. A rectangular lot contains 4.7 acres and is 220 feet wide. What is the depth of the lot?
   a. 1023.66 feet
   b. 930.60 feet
   c. 969.05 feet

d. 974.6 feet

76. The maximum amount of costs and expenses in making the loan covered by the California Real Property Loans Act that are paid by the borrower, exclusive of title charges and recording fees, is
a. 10% of the loan amount
b. 5% of the loan amount
c. $390
d. none of the above

77. An acceleration clause is
a. a clause in either a promissory note, a security instrument, or both that states that upon default the lender has the option of declaring the entire balance of outstanding principal and interest due and payable immediately
b. a provision in a loan that states that when the loan debt has been fully paid, the lender must release the property from the lien so that legal title free from the lien will be owned by the borrower
c. a clause in the promissory note, the security instrument, or both that states that the lender has the right to accelerate the loan if the secured property is sold or some other interest in the property is transferred
d. a cost-recovery clause in a promissory note

78. Which of the following terms least belongs with the others?
a. loan modification
b. trustee's sale
c. right of reinstatement
d. nonjudicial foreclosure

79. Between a typical mortgage and a typical deed of trust
a. the most important difference is the ability to modify the loan
b. the most important difference is the foreclosure process
c. the most important difference is the interest rate on the loan
d. the most important difference is the length of the loan term

80. California usury laws permit which, if any, of the following loans to charge any amount of interest that the market will bear?
a. seller carry back loans
b. loans negotiated by a real estate broker
c. both a and b

d. neither a nor b

81. A loan under which payments are sufficient to pay off the entire loan by the end of the loan term is called
    a. a balloon payment loan
    b. a negative amortized loan
    c. a fully amortized loan
    d. an adjustable-rate loan

82. In an assumption,
    a. the seller remains personally liable on the loan, but the purchaser is not personally liable on the loan
    b. the buyer agrees to be primarily liable on the loan
    c. there is no prepayment penalty
    d. the lender agrees to subordinate the loan

83. A clause in a deed trust that allows the beneficiary to declare the entire balance of the loan due and payable immediately if the borrower materially defaults on the loan is called
    a. due-on-sale clause
    b. acceleration clause
    c. defeasance clause
    d. either a or b

84. In a deed of trust, what clause permits the trustee to sell the property if the borrower defaults
    a. alienation
    b. power of sale
    c. due-on-sale
    d. assumption

85. Which of the following terms least belongs with the others?
    a. deficiency judgment
    b. due-on-sale clause
    c. judicial foreclosure

d. sheriff's sale

86. Determinants of a borrower's capacity to repay a loan include
   a. assets
   b. source of income
   c. purpose of loan
   d. both a and b

87. One of the primary concerns of the SAFE Act is with
   a. ensuring that new homes are built to the latest safety standards as set by the FHFA
   b. reducing mortgage fraud
   c. both a and b
   d. neither a nor b

88. Which of the following terms least belongs with the others?
   a. source of income
   b. property due diligence
   c. appraisal
   d. preliminary title report

89. PMI stands for
   a. primary mortgage insurance
   b. property mortgage insurance
   c. primary mortgage investment
   d. none of the above

90. The law requires lenders to provide borrowers with disclosures as to when PMI is no longer required on the borrowers' loans is referred to as
   a. Nationwide Mortgage Licensing Act
   b. Homeowner's Protection Act
   c. Federal Home Loan Protection Act
   d. none of the above

91. The completion of 20 hours of pre-license education is required in certain instances by the
   a. FHFA Licensing Act
   b. CLM Act
   c. SAFE Act

d. none of the above

92. One of the primary concerns of the SAFE Act is with
    a. improving the protection of residential loan borrowers
    b. ensuring that low LTV loans have PMI
    c. stabilizing the secondary mortgage market
    d. requiring that nonconforming loans cost more than conforming

93. Increasing the loan balance by adding in unpaid interest is referred to as
    a. balloon adjustment
    b. negative amortization
    c. partial amortization
    d. none of the above

94. What is the minimum number of active service days that qualifies a veteran for a CalVet loan?
    a. 60
    b. 90
    c. 181
    d. none of the above

95. Child support would likely be included in
    a. front-end ratio
    b. LTV
    c. PMI
    d. none of the above

96. Cost recovery is the recoupment of the purchase price of a property through
    a. capitalization depreciation
    b. deferred maintenance
    c. book depreciation
    d. preventive maintenance

97. A Form Report is also referred to as a
    a. Summary Report

b. Self-Contained Report
c. Restricted Use Report
d. Brief Report

98. A comparable has an inferior view to the view of the subject property. An appraiser using the sales comparison approach will
   a. adjust the sale price of the comparable up
   b. adjust the sale price of the comparable down
   c. make no adjustment for view
   d. adjust the sale price of the subject property down

99. The purpose of an appraisal is to
   a. defer maintenance
   b. recover the price of a property over a given time
   c. estimate the value of the property for a particular purpose
   d. determine the interest rate

100. A decrease in land value might result from
   a. the principle of cost recovery
   b. functional obsolescence
   c. principle of supply and demand
   d. book depreciation

101. Economic obsolescence generally is
   a. obsolescence resulting from outdated equipment
   b. obsolescence resulting from wear and tear of use
   c. curable depreciation
   d. incurable depreciation

102. A Self-Contained Report is also referred to as a
   a. Form Report
   b. Restricted Use Report
   c. Summary Report
   d. none of the above

103. The sales comparison approach most heavily relies on the
   a. principal of substitution
   b. principal of conformity

c. principle of balance

d. principle of competition

104. To help ascertain estate and gift taxes and to help ascertain the basis for depreciation in regard to income producing properties are not
    a. tax related activities
    b. potential purposes of an appraisal
    c. both a and b
    d. neither a nor b

105. The cost-to-cure method of calculating depreciation
    a. estimates the cost to cure the curable depreciation and subtracts it from the value of incurable depreciation
    b. calculates the accrued depreciation by dividing the cost of the improvement by its useful life
    c. calculates the accrued depreciation by dividing the cost of the improvement by the estimated useful life of a typical such improvement
    d. none of the above

106. An escrow agent is someone with whom
    a. the seller can feel safe depositing all or part of the purchase price before receiving the deed
    b. the buyer can feel safe depositing the deed before receiving the purchase price
    c. the lender can feel secure that none of its loan funds will be disbursed until the promissory note and the deed of trust are signed by the buyer
    d. all of the above

107. As the term is used in reference to escrow accounting, a debit is
    a. any item payable to a party
    b. any item deposited into escrow
    c. any escrow instruction relating to deposits of funds
    d. none of the above

108. A real estate broker who acts as an escrow agent for a real estate transaction

a. may accept escrow instructions that contain one or more blanks to be filled in after the signing of the instructions
b. need not deliver at the time of the signing of any escrow instruction a copy thereof to all persons signing the instruction
c. both a and b
d. neither a nor b

109. An escrow is
    a. settlement form mandated by RESPA for use in all purchases of owner-occupied residences of 1-4 dwelling units that use funds from institutional lenders regulated by the federal government
    b. a report to be submitted to the IRS to report the sale of real estate, giving the seller's name, Social Security number, and the gross sale proceeds
    c. the written instructions that specify all of the conditions that must be met before the escrow agent may release whatever was deposited to the rightful parties
    d. none of the above

110. A real estate broker must file a threshold report with the CalBRE if he or she engages in how many escrow activities in a calendar year?
    a. 5
    b. 4
    c. 3
    d. 2

111. An escrow agent is
    a. an employee of an escrow company
    b. a corporation licensed by the Bureau of Real Estate
    c. a real estate broker who refers a client to an escrow company
    d. none of the above

112. A real estate broker who is not licensed as an escrow agent
    a. may advertise that he or she can conduct escrow for any real estate transaction
    b. may conduct escrow for any real estate transaction
    c. may not conduct escrow for any real estate transaction
    d. none of the above

113. A binding contract between buyer and seller may be
    a. a deposit receipt
    b. escrow instructions
    c. either a or b
    d. neither a nor b

114. As the term is used in reference to escrow accounts, a credit is any
    a. item payable by a party
    b. item payable to a party
    c. item deposited into an escrow
    d. none of the above

115. Verifying that the title policy is in place and sending the original policy to the borrower is an act typically performed by the
    a. buyer
    b. seller
    c. lender
    d. none of the above

116. A gross lease is also referred to as a
    a. net lease
    b. fixed lease
    c. step-up lease
    d. ground lease

117. A lease extension
    a. is a continuation of tenancy under a new lease
    b. is a lease with a term not exceeding one month
    c. creates an estate at sufferance
    d. is a continuation of tenancy under the original lease

118. If a tenant complains to the health department that her apartment building is rat infested and the landlord refuses to take appropriate measures to remedy the problem, the landlord may give the tenant
    a. 30-day notice to terminate
    b. 30-day notice to terminate (or 60-day notice if the tenant has been in possession of the premises for over one year)

c. 90-day notice

d. none of the above

119. A lease for residential property that provides for an automatic extension of the lease if the tenant remains in possession after the expiration of the lease is voidable by the party who did not prepare the lease unless

a. the renewal or extension clause is in at least 10-point type

b. the renewal or extension clause is printed in at least eight-point boldface type and a recital of such clause is on the first page of the lease

c. the renewal or extension clause is in boldface type

d. none of the above

120. The Costa-Hawkins Rental Housing Act

a. places restrictions on local rent control ordinances as they pertain to rent

b. does not place restrictions on local rent control ordinances as they pertain to evictions

c. both a and b

d. neither a nor b

121. Bob's lease is a gross lease. What percent of the property taxes on the premises is Bob responsible for paying?

a. all of the property taxes

b. none of the property taxes

c. some percentage of the property taxes as provided in the lease

d. none of the above

122. If a tenant remains in possession of leased property after the expiration of the lease and the landlord accepts rent from the tenant, the tenancy is presumed to be

a. an estate at will

b. an estate at sufferance

c. under a renewed lease

d. a freehold interest

123. Constructive eviction arises from

a. acts of government authorities

b. breaches by a tenant
c. breaches by a landlord
d. any of the above

124. In the absence of a provision in the lease that states when rent is due, and in absence of a course of dealing between landlord and tenant, rent is due
    a. at the beginning of each month
    b. at the end of each month
    c. at the beginning of each week
    d. none of the above

125. Under the Costa-Hawkins Rental Housing Act
    a. there can be no rent restriction on rental units built after February 1, 1995
    b. there can be no control of rents for leases on single-family homes where the leases are entered into after January 1, 1996
    c. both a and b
    d. neither a nor b

126. The landmark case of *Jones v. Mayer* was held to be constitutional based on which Amendment to the U.S. Constitution?
    a. Fourteenth
    b. Thirteenth
    c. Twelfth
    d. First

127. A corporation formed or of availed of primarily for the purpose of holding title to improved real property either in fee simple or for a term of years is
    a. an undivided interest subdivision
    b. the community apartment project
    c. a residential unit owned in severalty, the boundaries of which are usually walls, floors, and ceilings, and an undivided interest in portions of the real property, such as halls, elevators, and recreational facilities

d. a stock cooperative

128. To be validly used, police power in the real estate context must
   a. not reduce the value of real estate to such an extent as to amount to confiscation
   b. apply similarly to all property similarly situated
   c. both a and b
   d. neither a nor b

129. A development (other than a condominium, community apartment project, or stock cooperative) consisting of lots or parcels owned separately and areas owned in common and reserved for the use of some or all the owners of the separate interests is
   a. a common interest development
   b. a standard development
   c. an undivided interest subdivision
   d. a parceled subdivision

130. A subdivider who wishes to begin a marketing effort before a final public report is issued may request what?
   a. an amended public report
   b. a preliminary public report
   c. a tentative map
   d. an interim report

131. An amendment to a zoning ordinance that property owners may request if they feel that their area has been improperly zoned is referred to as
   a. nonconforming use
   b. conditional use
   c. variance
   d. none of the above

132. Condominiums are not regulated under the
   a. Subdivided Land Law
   b. Subdivision Map Act
   c. both a and b
   d. neither a nor b

133. If a subdivision located outside of the United States is offered in California, the offeror must
   a. register the project with the CalBRE
   b. include certain disclaimers in advertising and sales contracts
   c. both a and b
   d. neither a nor b

134. Of the following, which is not an exercise of police power?
   a. zoning ordinances
   b. building codes
   c. subdivision laws
   d. none of the above

135. The Contractors' State License Law
   a. is a California state law that provides local governments with the authority to correct blighted conditions in areas within their jurisdictions
   b. is a California state law that, with certain exceptions, requires that every building contractor must be licensed by the Contractors' State License Board
   c. is a California state law that requires state and local agencies to consider and respond to the environmental effects of private and public development projects
   d. none of the above

136. After the expiration of the 5-year redemption period on delinquent taxes the taxpayer
   a. may not redeem the property
   b. may redeem the property within two years
   c. may redeem the property until the property is sold
   d. may redeem the property within one year

137. A business in which the taxpayer does not materially participate is
   a. a possible source of passive income
   b. a source of ordinary income
   c. both a and b

d. neither a nor b

138. The fiscal tax year in California ends on
    a. December 31
    b. February 15
    c. June 30
    d. April 15

139. To qualify as a 1031 exchange, it might be possible to exchange a farm for property to be used as
    a. a principal place of residence
    b. rental property
    c. a vacation or second home
    d. none of the above

140. Which of the following phrases least belongs with the others?
    a. 1% of the "full cash value"
    b. special assessments
    c. up to 2% per year increase
    d. CPI

141. The redemption period that begins after a tax collector publishes an intent to sell is
    a. 5 years
    b. 4 years
    c. 3 years
    d. 1 year

142. The two sources of passive income are
    a. rental activity and salaries
    b. rental activity and dividends
    c. rental activity and gains on stocks and bonds
    d. none of the above

143. Under a tax postponement program
    a. repayment of all postponed taxes must be made when the property is sold

b. repayment of all postponed taxes must be made when the owner of the property reaches the age of 62

c. the postponed taxes need not be repaid if the owner reaches the age of 90

d. none of the above

144. It is possible to qualify as a 1031 exchange if an apartment building is exchanged for a property to be used as a
    a. personal residence
    b. vacation home
    c. second home
    d. none of the above

145. Proposition 13 states that the maximum ad valorem tax on real property shall include what percent of the property's "full cash value"?
    a. 1%
    b. 2%
    c. up to 2%, as long as it does not exceed the CPI
    d. none of the above

146. The amount of heat required to raise 1 pound of water from 39°F to 40°F is
    a. an R-value
    b. a BTU
    c. an SEER
    d. an EER

147. The ratio of the cooling capacity to power consumption of a central air conditioner is called
    a. SEER
    b. EER
    c. R-value
    d. BTU

148. The horizontal board placed on edge at the apex of a roof to which the upper ends of the rafters are attached is the
    a. collar beam

b. dormer
c. flue
d. none of the above

149. A newly built manufactured home
   a. must be registered with the Department of Housing and Community Development before it can be sold in California
   b. comes out of the factory as personal property
   c. both a and b
   d. neither a nor b

150. A real estate broker may sell a manufactured home that
   a. has been installed on a permanent foundation
   b. has been registered with the Department of Housing and Community Development
   c. either a or b
   d. neither a nor b

Answers to Practice Exam #1

Note: If you would like to obtain a deeper understanding of the real estate principles behind the following answers, consult the textbook *California Real Estate Principles and License Preparation, 2ⁿᵈ Edition*, which is available both in print and Kindle formats on Amazon.com. The author, Jim Bainbridge, is a graduate of Harvard Law School, a member of the California Bar, and a licensed California real estate broker.

1.   c. Ordinarily, debt cancellation results in both the IRS and the California Franchise Tax Board (FTB) treating the amount of debt canceled as income and taxed accordingly. However, in a September 19, 2013 letter to Senator Barbara Boxer, the IRS stated: "We believe that a homeowner's obligation under the anti-deficiency provision of section 580e of the CCP would be a nonrecourse obligation to the extent that, for federal income tax purposes, the homeowner will not have cancellation of indebtedness income." Shortly after the IRS issued this letter, the FTB also issued a letter stating that short sales made pursuant to CCP §580e would not be subject to state income taxation.

2.   b. Upon the sale of real estate, the landowner's rights to the minerals that lie beneath the property automatically pass with the deed, unless specifically excluded.

3.   d. A nonprofit company created to provide water supplies for property owners in a specific district is called a mutual water company.

4.   c. Both an easement appurtenant an easement in gross encumber a servient tenement.

5.   b. An easement may be created by prescription, necessity, or express grant.

6.   b. Drawing a diagram for these types of problems is usually helpful. Because a section contains 640 acres, the W 1/2 of the NW 1/4 contains 640 acres ÷ 8 = 80 acres. Similarly, the SE 1/4 of the N 1/2 contains 640 acres ÷ 8 = 80 acres, and the SE 1/4 of the SE 1/4 of the E 1/2 contains 640 acres ÷ 32 = 20 acres, giving us a grand total of 180 acres.

7.   d. An easement in gross is an easement that benefits a legal person rather than other land. In this example, the cable company probably does not own adjacent land so there would not be a dominant tenement.

8. c. A condition subsequent is a condition that, upon its occurrence, can result in the forfeiture of an interest in property back to the grantor.

9. c. The branch would be an encroachment, which would allow Jane to cut and remove the branch up to the property line but not to go onto Bob's property to cut down the tree.

10. a. The transfer of real property is completed by the delivery of a deed.

11. d. If at the end of a life estate, the future interest arises in someone other than the grantor, the residue of the estate is called a remainder.

12. a. A condition subsequent would likely be found in a deed.

13. b. This lease is for a definite fixed term and is therefore an estate for years.

14. c. A life estate is an estate of inheritance.

15. c. The four types of leasehold estates differ according to their characteristics, creation, duration, limitation on term, and termination.

16. c. A tenancy for years is a leasehold that continues for a definite fixed period of time, measured in days, months, or years.

17. d. A tenancy for years is a leasehold that continues for a definite fixed period of time, which may exceed 49 years.

18. b. A lease for 33 days is an estate for years because it is for a definite period.

19. d. An estate at will can be terminated by the landlord upon giving a 30-day notice to quit.

20. b. A lease in real estate conveys to the tenant an exclusive right to possess.

21. b. If the decedent leaves two or more children and a spouse or domestic partner, 1/3 goes to the spouse or domestic partner, 2/3 is divided equally among the children. In this example, 1/2 of 2/3 is 1/3.

22. c. A late bid must be at least 10% higher than the first $10,000 plus 5% higher than the balance of the highest bid being considered. Therefore, in this example the late bid must be for at least $95,000.

23. c. Avulsion is a process that occurs when a river or stream suddenly carries away a part of a bank and deposits it downstream, either on the same or opposite bank. Alluvium is an addition to land acquired by the gradual accumulation of soil through the action of water. *Be careful when the word "false" appears in a question.*

24.   b. Avulsion occurs when a river or stream suddenly carries away a part of a bank and deposits it downstream, either on the same or opposite bank. The owner of the carried-away property may, within one year, reclaim his or her property; otherwise, it becomes part of the property onto which it settled.

25.   b. Abandonment, adverse possession, and prescription are ways in which real property or its use may be acquired due to occupancy.

26.   c. A grant deed must be legally delivered to be valid, but it need not be acknowledged or recorded.

27.   b. Eminent domain is the right of the state to take, through due process proceedings, private property for public use upon payment of just compensation.

28.   d. A valid deed need not be dated, recorded, or signed by a grantee.

29.   b. Eminent domain proceedings are often referred to as condemnation proceedings.

30.   b. A person who dies intestate dies without leaving a will.

31.   b. A corporation cannot be a joint tenant, and we have no information that B and C have formed any kind of partnership, so B and C would be tenants in common.

32.   c. A joint tenancy may be terminated either by agreement among the joint tenants through a voluntary partition, or, if no voluntary agreement can be reached, by a judicial determination after the filing of a partition action by one or more of the joint tenants.

33.   d. Tenants in common have an undivided interest in the property and may not commit waste against the property.

34.   d. Joint tenants have a right of survivorship, so B's inclusion of her interest in the property in her will has no legal effect. C has no interest in the property.

35.   c. Although there is only one title to property held as community property, each spouse owns one-half interest in the property.

36.   b. Bob may dispose of a tenancy in common interest that is not part of community property. He may not dispose by will all of the community property.

37.   d. Jane and Susan can own the property as joint tenants or as tenants in common, but not as community property because they are not married.

38.   b. The most important characteristic of joint tenancy is considered to be right of survivorship.

39.   b. Because joint tenancy has right of survivorship, a joint tenant may not will his or her interest to another.

40.   c. Jane owned the property as separate property before marriage, and unless otherwise agreed, the property would remain her separate property following marriage.

41.   a. Though a notice of pendency of action is not a lien, it serves as constructive notice to prospective purchasers or encumbrancers of the property identified in the notice of pendency of action of the pending lawsuit, and such person would, therefore, be bound by any judgment resulting from the lawsuit.

42.   a. An attachment lien cannot be foreclosed on

43.   c. To obtain an attachment lien, the amount in controversy must be $500 or more.

44.   a. A judgment lien is a general lien.

45.   a. A preliminary notice must be given within 20 days after first providing the labor or materials for a work of improvement.

46.   b. Liens placed on real property to enforce the collection of real property taxes are specific liens, affecting only in the property against which the lien attaches.

47.   c. Lis pendens and preliminary notice are terms related to mechanics liens.

48.   d. Judgment liens, abstracts of judgment, and involuntary liens are all consequences of involuntary actions against debtors.

49.   d. Of these three, only an automatic homestead need not be recorded to be valid.

50.   b. A notice of nonresponsibility is a written notice that a property owner may record and post on the property to shield the owner from any liability for a work of improvement on the property that a lessee or a purchaser under a land sales contract authorized.

51.   c. An emancipated minor is a minor who has been validly married (even if the marriage has been terminated), is serving in the military, or has been declared emancipated by court order.

52.   d. Mutual consent (often referred to as a "meeting of the minds") is usually evidenced by an offer of one party that manifests contractual intention, and by an acceptance by the other party. Menace refers to a threat of duress or of injury to person or property of a person.

53.   a. Mutual consent (often referred to as a "meeting of the minds") is usually evidenced by an offer of one party that manifests contractual intention and by an acceptance by the other party.

54.   b. A counter offer is effective upon receipt.

55.   c. An offer can be terminated by a revocation of the offer by the offeror or by a rejection of the offer by the offeree.

56.   d. A counter offer by an offeree terminates the offeror's offer and presents a new offer to the offeror.

57.   c. A voidable contract is a contract that, at the request of one party only, may be declared unenforceable, but is valid until it is so declared.

58.   c. In California, the statute of limitations for written contracts generally is 4 years.

59.   b. In California, oral contracts to lease for a period of one year or less need not be in writing.

60.   d. An executed contract is a contract that has been fully performed by all parties.

61.   b. The equal dignities rule is a principle of agency law that requires the same formality to create the agency as is required for the act(s) the agent is hired to perform.

62.   c. Though agency by implication and ostensible agency appear to be much the same, the crucial difference is that in agency by implication the supposed agent is found to owe agency duties to the principal, whereas in ostensible agency, the agent and the principal are found to be liable for their actions to a third party.

63.   a. State and federal taxing authorities recognize a salesperson *as an independent contractor* by not requiring the employing broker to withhold from the salesperson's paychecks for items such as federal or state income taxes, Medicare, Social Security, or unemployment insurance, as long as there is a written contract between the broker and the salesperson that clearly states that the employment relationship between the broker and the salesperson is one between an employer and an independent contractor.

64.   c. Though a principal is liable to third parties for the actions of an agent who acts within his or her authority, no liability is incurred by a principal for the acts of an agent beyond the scope of the agent's actual or ostensible authority. A third party who is aware that he or she is dealing with an authorized agent has the duty to ascertain the purpose and scope of the agency.

65. b. Commingling results from the failure to properly segregate the funds belonging to the agent from the funds received and held on behalf of the seller or buyer.

66. a. California's antitrust law is based upon the Cartwright Act.

67. b. Both an employed person and an independent contractor may work a few or many hours, depending in the first case on the wishes of the employer and in the second case on the independent contractor himself or herself.

68. a. Though a listing agent owes a potential buyer the duty of fair dealing and must give numerous disclosures to a potential buyer, the listing agent is not a potential buyer's fiduciary unless the agent becomes a dual agent representing both the seller and the buyer.

69. c. In this scenario, Sally and Bob may be found guilty of implicitly fixing commission rates.

70. a. An agency relationship by implication can be created by an unauthorized agent who acts as if he or she is the agent of a principal, and this principal reasonably believes that the unauthorized agent is acting as his or her actual agent.

71. a. $4,500,000 at 9%/yr. = $405,000/yr. $405,000/yr. ÷ 12 mo./yr. = $33,750.

72. c. ¼ acre is 43,560 ft.² ÷ 4 = 10,890 ft.².
10,890 ft.² x $17/ ft.² = $185,130. Susan's commission was 4% of $185,130 = $7,405.20

73. d. The annual rental income is $17,000/mo. x 12 mo./yr. = $204,000/yr. 41% of $204,000/yr. = $83,640/yr..

74. d. ($3,895.83 x 12) ÷ 5 1/2% = $849,999.27, which represents 85% of the cost of the house. Therefore, the cost of the house is $849,999.27 ÷ 85% = $999,999 (rounded).

75. b. There are 4.7 acres x 43,560 ft.²/acre = 204,732 ft.². 204,732 ft.² ÷ 220 ft. = 930.6 ft.

76. d. The maximum amount of costs and expenses in making the loan that are paid by the borrower, exclusive of actual title charges and recording fees, is limited to 5% of the principal amount of the loan or $390, whichever is greater, but in no event can they exceed $700.

77. a. An acceleration clause is a clause in either a promissory note, a security instrument, or both that states that upon default the lender has the option of declaring the entire balance of outstanding principal and interest due and payable immediately.

78.   a. A trustee's sale is a nonjudicial sale in which the borrower has a right of reinstatement up to 5 business days prior to the sale.

79.   b. The foreclosure typically used in a mortgage is a judicial foreclosure; under a deed of trust, it is a nonjudicial foreclosure.

80.   c. California usury laws exempt seller carry back loans and loans negotiated by real estate brokers.

81.   c. A fully amortized loan is a loan whereby the installment payments are sufficient to pay off the entire loan by the end of the loan term.

82.   b. In an assumption, the buyer agrees to be primarily liable on the loan.

83.   b. A clause in a deed of trust that allows the beneficiary to declare the entire balance of the loan due and payable immediately is called an acceleration clause, which can be violated by any material default, including nonpayment of taxes, hazard insurance, etc.

84.   b. A power of sale clause is a clause contained in most trust deeds that permits the trustee to foreclose on, and sell, the secured property without going to court.

85.   b. A judicial foreclosure is completed by a sheriff's sale and may result in a deficiency judgment being given to the creditor.

86.   d. A borrower's capacity to repay a loan is determined in part by the borrower's assets and source of income.

87.   b. The SAFE Act was designed to improve consumer protection and reduce mortgage fraud by setting minimum standards for the licensing and registration of mortgage loan originators.

88.   a. Property due diligence, appraisals, and preliminary title reports are components of property information that a loan processor assembles.

89.   d. PMI is an acronym for private mortgage insurance.

90.   b. The Homeowner's Protection Act requires lenders disclose to borrowers when the borrowers' mortgages no longer require PMI.

91.   c. The completion of 20 hours of pre-license education is required for state-licensed MLOs by the SAFE Act.

92.   a. The SAFE Act was designed to improve consumer protection and reduce mortgage fraud by setting minimum standards for the licensing and registration of mortgage loan originators.

93.   b. Increasing the loan balance by adding in unpaid interest is referred to as negative amortization.

94.　b. A minimum number of 90 days active service is required to qualify a veteran for a CalVet loan.

95.　d. Monthly child support payments would be included in back-end ratios.

96.　c. Cost recovery is the recoupment of the purchase price of a property through book depreciation.

97.　a. A Summary Report is also referred to as a Form Report.

98.　a. In the sales comparison approach, the appraiser adjusts the sales price of comparable properties by estimating what these properties would have sold for if they had had the same features as the subject property. Therefore, because the subject property has a better view, the sale price of the comparable in this case would be adjusted up.

99.　c. To estimate the value of a property for a particular purpose is the purpose of an appraisal.

100.　c. Land prices are subject to supply and demand but not to functional obsolescence or to cost recovery.

101.　d. Economic obsolescence is usually beyond the control of a property owner and is therefore incurable.

102.　d. A Self-Contained Report is also referred to as a Narrative Report.

103.　a. The principle of substitution holds that buyers are generally unwilling to pay more for a property than for a substitute (a comparable with appropriate adjustments) property in the area.

104.　d. Helping to ascertain estate and gift taxes and the basis for depreciation in regard to income producing properties *are* tax related and potentially purposes of an appraisal. [Be careful if the word "not" appears in questions.]

105.　d. The cost-to-cure method calculates depreciation by estimating the cost of curing the curable depreciation and *adding* to it the value of the incurable depreciation.

106.　c. Answers a and b have buyer and seller reversed.

107.　d. As the term is used in reference to escrow accounting, a debit is an item payable *by* a party.

108.　d. A real estate broker who acts as an escrow agent for a real estate transaction must not accept escrow instructions that contain one or more blanks to be filled in after the signing of the instructions and must not fail to deliver, at the time of the signing any escrow instruction, a copy thereof to all persons signing the instruction.

109. d. An escrow is a neutral depository in which something of value is held by an impartial third party (called the escrow agent) until all conditions specified in the escrow instructions have been fully performed.

110. a. A real estate broker who engages in 5 or more escrow activities in a calendar year must file a threshold report with the CalBRE.

111. d. An escrow agent is an impartial agent who holds possession of written instruments and deposits until all of the conditions of escrow have been fully performed.

112. d. A real estate broker not licensed as an escrow agent may serve as an escrow agent for any real estate transaction in which the broker represents the buyer or seller or is a party to the transaction and performs acts that require a real estate license.

113. c. A binding contract between buyer and seller can be in any legal form, including a deposit receipt or escrow instructions.

114. b. As the term is used in reference to escrow accounts, a credit is any item payable to a party.

115. d. Verifying that the title policy is in place and sending the original policy to the borrower is an act typically performed by the escrow agent.

116. b. A gross lease is also referred to as a fixed lease.

117. d. A lease extension is a continuation of tenancy under the original lease.

118. d. Such an attempted eviction referred to in answers a-c is illegal and is referred to as a retaliatory eviction.

119. d. A lease for residential property that provides for an automatic extension of the lease if the tenant remains in possession after the expiration of the lease, or if the tenant fails to give notice of the tenant's intention not to renew or extend, is voidable by the party who did not prepare the lease, unless the renewal or extension clause is printed in at least 8-point boldface type and a recital of such clause is printed in at least 8-point boldface type above the tenant's signature line.

120. c. The Costa-Hawkins Rental Housing Act places restrictions on local rent control ordinances as they pertain to rent, though not as they pertain to evictions.

121. b. A gross lease is a lease under which the tenant pays a fixed rental amount, and the landlord pays all of the operating expenses for the premises, including taxes.

122. c. If a tenant remains in possession of the leased property after the expiration of the lease and the landlord accepts rent from the tenant, the lease is presumed to have been extended or renewed on the same terms

and for the same time, not exceeding one month if the rent under the original lease is payable monthly, or in any case not exceeding one year.

123. c. Constructive eviction is a breach by the landlord of the covenant of habitability or quiet enjoyment.

124. d. In the absence of a provision in the lease that states when rent is due, and in the absence of a course of dealing between landlord and tenant rent is due at the termination of the successive lease periods, which may be different from a month.

125. c. Under the Costa-Hawkins Rental Housing act there can be no rent restriction on rental units built after February 1, 1995 and there can be no control of rents for leases on single-family homes where the leases are entered into after January 1, 1996.

126. b. In 1968, the United States Supreme Court held in the landmark case, *Jones v. Mayor*, that the Civil Rights Act of 1866 was constitutional (based on the Thirteenth Amendment) and that it prohibited all racial discrimination, whether private or public, in the sale or rental of property.

127. d. A stock cooperative is a corporation formed or of availed of primarily for the purpose of holding title to improved real property either in fee simple or for a term of years.

128. c. To be validly used (i.e., constitutional), police power in the real estate context must be reasonably related to protecting the health, safety, or general welfare of the public; apply similarly to all property similarly situated; and not reduce the value of the real estate to such an extent as to amount to confiscation (in which case eminent domain must be used and compensation paid to the property owner).

129. a. A common interest development is a subdivision in which purchasers own or lease a separate lot, unit, or interest, and have an undivided interest or membership in a portion of the common area of the subdivision, of which a planned development is a type.

130. b. A subdivider who wishes to begin a marketing effort before a final public report is issued may request that a preliminary public report be issued.

131. d. An amendment to a zoning ordinance that property owners may request if they feel that their area has been improperly zoned is referred to as a rezoning amendment.

132. d. Both the Subdivided Lands Law and the Subdivision Map act regulate condominium projects.

133. b. If a subdivision is located outside of the United States, the offeror need not register with the CalBRE, but sales contracts and advertising must contain certain disclosures.

134. d. Zoning ordinances, building codes, and subdivision laws are all instances of the use of police power.

135. b. The Contractors' State License Law is a California state law that, with certain exceptions, requires that every building contractor must be licensed by the Contractors' State License Board.

136. c. Until the county tax collector sells the property at public auction, the tax payer may still redeem the property by paying all delinquent taxes and penalties.

137. a. As a general rule, passive losses are deductible only to the extent of passive income. There are only two sources of passive income: (1) rental activity and (2) a business in which the taxpayer does not materially participate.

138. c. The fiscal tax year in California ends on June 30.

139. b. To qualify as a 1031 exchange, the property must be of "like kind." In general, this means that any real property not for personal use can be exchanged for any other real property not for personal use (for example, a farm can be exchanged for an apartment building.

140. b. Proposition 13 places a maximum ad valorem tax on real property equal to 1% of the "full cash value" plus a maximum increase of the assessed value of up to 2% per year, as long as the annual increase does not exceed the Consumer Price Index (CPI). Proposition 13 applies only to ad valorem real estate taxes, not to special taxes or assessments that impose a tax not based on the value of the real estate.

141. a. The redemption period that begins after a tax collector publishes an intent to sell is 5 years.

142. d. There are only two sources of passive income: (1) rental activity and (2) a business in which the taxpayer does not materially participate.

143. a. Repayment of all postponed taxes has to be made when the property is sold or title transferred.

144. d. To qualify as a 1031 exchange, the property must be of like kind. In general, this means that any property held for business use or investment can be exchanged for any other like-kind property held for business use or investment (for example, a farm can be exchanged for an apartment building).

145. a. Basically, Proposition 13 places a maximum ad valorem tax on real property equal to 1% of the "full cash value" plus a maximum increase of the assessed value of up to 2% per year, as long as the annual increase does not exceed the Consumer Price Index (CPI).

146. b. A BTU is a measure of heating (or cooling) capacity equivalent to the amount of heat required to raise the temperature of 1 pound of water 1° Fahrenheit (from 39°F to 40°F).

147. a. SEER is an efficiency rating that states the ratio of the cooling capacity (how many BTUs per hour) to the power drawn (in watts) for central air conditioners.

148. d. A ridgeboard is the horizontal board placed on edge at the apex of a roof to which the upper ends of the rafters are attached.

149. c. A newly built manufactured home comes out of the factory as personal property and must be registered with the Department of Housing and Community Development before it can be sold in California.

150. c. A person who sells manufactured homes must possess a valid Department of Housing and Community Development (HCD) Occupational License. An exception to this requirement is that real estate brokers licensed by the CalBRE may sell manufactured homes that have been registered with the HCD or have been installed on a permanent foundation pursuant to Health and Safety Code §18551.

Practice Exam #2:

1. All easements can be terminated by
    a. the dominant tenement and servient tenement becoming owned by the same person
    b. by nonuse for a period of 5 years
    c. both a and b
    d. neither a nor b

2. Which of the following do not constitute real property?
    a. things attached to the land by roots, such as trees
    b. things embedded in the land, such as walls
    c. both a and b
    d. neither a nor b

3. Which of the following is (are) false?
    a. growing crops that are produced through a tenant farmer's labor are called encroachments
    b. a prescriptive easement cannot be terminated through nonuse
    c. both a and b
    d. neither a nor b

4. Tests of a fixture include
    a. whether the person who, because of mistake of law or fact, encroached upon the land in good faith
    b. the intent of the person attaching the item
    c. both a and b
    d. neither a nor b

5. Which of the following is (are) true?
    a. a legal action to recover possession of real property from a person who is not legally entitled to possess it, such as to remove an encroachment or to evict a defaulting buyer or tenant is called an ejectment
    b. the support that soil receives from the land adjacent to it is called subjacent support
    c. both a and b
    d. neither a nor b

6. In order for an easement in gross to exist, there must be

108

a. a servient tenement

b. a dominant tenement

c. both a and b

d. neither a nor b

7. A deed restriction would be created by
    a. a local zoning commission
    b. a state statute
    c. the grantor
    d. a local planning commission

8. Which of the following is a freehold estate?
    a. estate at will
    b. tenancy at sufferance
    c. estate for years
    d. none of the above

9. In real estate, "bundle of rights" refers to rights or interests, including the right to
    a. possess
    b. exclude from others
    c. encumber
    d. all of the above

10. For seven years now, Jane has been using, without Bob's permission, a shortcut over Bob's property to walk to a bus stop. Jane probably has
    a. a prescriptive easement
    b. an easement by necessity
    c. a license
    d. an adjacent right

11. A life tenant is obligated to act reasonably to avoid
    a. an increase in rent
    b. wasting
    c. lateral support
    d. the law of capture

12. Which of the following terms least belongs with the others?
    a. life estate
    b. estate from period to period
    c. estate at will
    d. estate for years

13. Among the following, which is the main distinguishing feature between a license and a lease?
    a. duration
    b. exclusivity of possession
    c. whether the contract is written or oral
    d. consideration paid

14. If ownership of the property that a licensee has permission to use is transferred
    a. the license may be terminated upon giving a 3-day notice
    b. the license may be terminated upon giving a 30-day notice
    c. the license is revoked
    d. none of the above

15. Which of the following is (are) false?
    a. a reversion is the residue of a freehold estate where at the end of the estate, the future interest reverts to the grantor
    b. a remainder is the residue of a freehold estate where, at the end of the estate, the future interest arises in a third person
    c. a license to use is a personal right to use property on an exclusive basis
    d. all of the above

16. If Susan dies before Joe, an estate in which Susan granted to Joe an estate for his life
    a. ceases to exist
    b. vests in Joe's heirs
    c. reverts to Susan's heirs
    d. none of the above

17. A freehold estate is also known as
    a. an estate at will
    b. an estate in full
    c. an estate for years

d. none of the above

18. A grants to B a life estate for the life of C. A
   a. is a remainderman
   b. is a lessor
   c. has a reversionary interest
   d. none of the above

19. A less-than-freehold estate may be
   a. a fee simple be feasible
   b. a leasehold estate
   c. an estate at term
   d. none of the above

20. Of the following, which is not an estate?
   a. a fee simple defeasible
   b. a lease
   c. a fee simple absolute
   d. none of the above

21. To acquire title to property by adverse possession,
   a. the possession must be for at least 5 years during the prior 10-year period
   b. the possession must be exclusive and hostile to the owner
   c. both a and b
   d. neither a nor b

22. To acquire a prescriptive easement
   a. the possession or use must be hostile to the owner
   b. there must be a claim of right or color of title
   c. both a and b
   d. neither a nor b

23. Which of the following terms least belongs with the others?
   a. foreclosure sale
   b. partition action
   c. public dedication
   d. sheriff's sale

24. Which of the following is (are) false?
   a. eminent domain is an exercise of police power
   b. compensation need not be made as part of the exercise eminent domain
   c. both a and b
   d. neither a nor b

25. Most individuals acquire real property by means of
   a. a grant deed
   b. a gift deed
   c. inheritance
   d. reversion

26. Which of the following is incorrect?
   a. acre = 43,650 square feet
   b. a section = 640 acres
   c. mile = 5,280 feet
   d. rod = 16.5 feet

27. Escheat is
   a. estate tax paid to the state
   b. what happens if your will is declared invalid
   c. what happens if you die without a will
   d. none of the above

28. A warranty deed conveys
   a. a warranty of good title
   b. after-acquired interests
   c. a warranty that the grantor owns the property
   d. all of the above

29. After a sheriff's sale, the purchaser receives a
   a. sheriff's deed
   b. quitclaim deed
   c. grant deed
   d. trust deed

30. If a broker was involved in the probate sale of a decedent's estate property, the broker will likely receive
    a. the going commission rate in that area
    b. 3%
    c. 5%
    d. whatever commission the court approves

31. Separate property excluded from community property includes
    a. property inherited during marriage
    b. rents from separately owned property
    c. both a and b
    d. neither a nor b

32. John and Susan are married. John uses money he earned during the marriage to buy a car for Susan as a birthday present. The car is
    a. John's separate property
    b. Susan's separate property
    c. community property of John and Susan
    d. none of the above

33. Bob and Susan own a house has community property. Bob takes out a loan and signs a mortgage against the house.
    a. the mortgage is valid against the house if Susan told Bob he could do what he did
    b. the mortgage is valid against the house whether Susan knew about the transfer or not
    c. the mortgage is not valid against the house unless Susan agreed to the mortgage in writing
    d. both a and b

34. Which of the following is (are) false?
    a. no deed needs to be signed by the grantee(s) to be valid as long as the grantor signs of the deed
    b. if a spouse mixes (commingles) his or her separate property to such an extent that a court cannot distinguish or trace which is which, the result will be that it all becomes community property
    c. both a and b
    d. neither a nor b

35. When a partner dies

113

a. title to the property rests entirely in the surviving partners
b. the partner's estate or heirs acquire no direct interest in the property of the partnership or in its management. The decedent's estate or heirs do, however, have a right to an accounting and a share of the partnership profits and value upon dissolution
c. both a and b
d. neither a nor b

36. Susan, a teacher, saved $20,000 during her marriage to Joe, an unemployed, bitter, and not very pleasant fellow. The divorce court will likely award Joe what portion of the $20,000?
a. $20,000
b. $10,000
c. $5000
d. $0

37. A corporation may not hold title in real property as
a. community property
b. joint tenancy
c. tenancy in common
d. either a or b

38. Without contrary evidence, it is presumed that married couples and registered domestic partners hold title in property as
a. tenants in common
b. community property
c. joint tenants
d. community property with right of survivorship

39. Jane and Bob are neither married nor registered domestic partners. If together they acquire a condo and keep ownership in it for seven years, title to the condo is presumed to be held as
a. tenants in common
b. joint tenants
c. community property
d. community property with right of survivorship

40. Which kind of property is usually subject to disposition by a will?

a. tenancy in common
b. community property
c. joint tenancy
d. both a and b

41. A notice of cessation may be recorded by the owner if there has been a continuous cessation of labor on the work of improvement for at least how many days prior to the recordation?
a. 45
b. 30
c. 25
d. 10

42. Which of the following is (are) false?
a. the holder of a mechanics lien must file a foreclosure action within 60 days after recordation of the lien
b. a notice of completion must be recorded within 30 days of the completion of a work of improvement
c. both a and b
d. neither a nor b

43. Which of the following is (are) true?
a. a notice of responsibility must be posted and recorded by the owner within 10 days of discovery of the work of improvement
b. the order in which lien holders are paid is known as lien priority
c. both a and b
d. neither a nor b

44. All mechanics liens relating to the same work of improvement
a. have equal priority
b. each mechanics lien holder is entitled to collect his or her pro rata share of the work furnished
c. both a and b
d. neither a nor b

45. The amount of protection California homestead law provides is
a. $75,000 for an individual
b. $175,000 if the homeowner is 55 years of age or older and single with an annual income of $15,000 or less, and the sale is an *involuntary* sale
c. both a and b

d. neither a nor b

46. If the owner does not file a notice of completion or a notice of cessation, how long after the completion of work does a subcontractor have to file a mechanics lien?
a. 10 days
b. 20 days
c. 30 days
d. 90 days

47. A direct contractor has how many days after first providing labor or material to a work of improvement to serve a preliminary notice on a construction lender?
a. 10
b. 20
c. 30
d. 60

48. A subcontractor has how many days after first providing labor or material to a work of improvement to file a preliminary notice?
a. 20
b. 30
c. 16
d. 90

49. Chronologically, which of the following is likely to happen?
a. abstract of judgment, lis pendens, writ of execution
b. attachment lien, writ of execution, judgment lien
c. lis pendens, judgment lien, writ of execution
d. mechanics lien, preliminary notice, foreclosure

50. A wage earner has how many days after first providing the labor or material to a work of improvement to file a preliminary notice?
a. 10
b. 20
c. 30

d. none of the above

51. Which of the following is (are) false?
   a. the revocation of an offer by an offeree terminates an offer
   b. death or incompetence of the offeror terminates an offer
   c. both a and b
   d. neither a nor b

52. Which of the following is (are) true?
   a. a valid contract must have lawful consideration
   b. a valid contract must have a lawful object
   c. if the contract has several objects, some of which are valid, the contract would normally be valid and enforced as to the lawful objects only
   d. all of the above

53. Consideration for a contract
   a. must be of essentially equal value to what is given in exchange for the consideration
   b. can consist of a forbearance
   c. both a and b
   d. neither a nor b

54. Under the California statute of frauds
   a. certain contracts are invalid, unless they, or some note or memorandum thereof, are in writing and subscribed by the party to be charged or by the party's agent
   b. contracts that are covered by the statute and that fail to be in writing, are not void but are unenforceable
   c. both a and b
   d. neither a nor b

55. Which of the following is (are) false?
   a. an agreement that by its terms is not to be performed within a year of its making need not be in writing
   b. an agreement that authorizes a broker to lease property for more than one year need not be in writing
   c. both a and b
   d. neither a nor b

56. To be valid and binding a contract
   a. must be in writing

b. must have a lawful object

c. the parties must be capable

d. both b and c

57. Joe makes an offer on May 15 to purchase Janet's house. The offer states that it will remain open and irrevocable for 1 week only. Joe can revoke his offer

a. only on May 15 or after May 22

b. only after May 22

c. at any time unless, prior to his revocation, he receives an acceptance from Janet before the expiration of the offer

d. never, because the offer was in writing

58. A counteroffer by an offeree

a. terminates the original offeror's offer

b. presents an offer to the original offeror

c. usually constitutes a qualified acceptance

d. both a and b

59. Of the following, which is not an essential element of a contract?

a. parol evidence

b. a writing evidencing a contract

c. consent of the parties

d. both a and b

60. Susan signed a listing agreement with Janet (and with no one else) and keeps the right to sell the property herself without paying Janet a commission. This is probably an example of

a. an open listing

b. an exclusive agency listing

c. an exclusive authorization and right to sell listing

d. a voidable listing

61. A post-dated check is a

a. promissory note

b. promise to pay

c. a negotiable instrument

d. cash equivalent

62. A broker's trust fund bank account must meet which, if any, of the following criteria?
   a. maintained in an account insured by the FDIC
   b. the broker's name must not be designated as the trustee for the account
   c. both a and b
   d. neither a nor b

63. Of the following, which if any are exceptions to the rule against commingling funds in a broker's trust account?
   a. the broker may keep no more than $200 of his personal funds in the account to pay service charges on the account
   b. the broker must, within 30 days of receiving a commission into the trust account, withdraw the amount of the commission from the account
   c. b but not a
   d. both a and b

64. After acceptance of an offer, the earnest money deposit
   a. may not be refunded by an agent or a subagent of the seller without the express written permission of the buyer
   b. may be given to the seller only if the seller expressly so provides in writing
   c. both a and b
   d. neither a nor b

65. Broker Sally had a deal fall through between her principal and the buyer, who had given a deposit. Both her principal and the buyer are now demanding that Sally give the deposit to them. Both are threatening to sue her.
   a. Sally should give the deposit to her principal, to whom she owes a fiduciary relationship
   b. Sally should return the deposit to the buyer because the deal fell through
   c. Sally should hold on to the deposit and defend against lawsuits by both her principal and the buyer
   d. Sally should file an interpleader action

66. A broker may use which of the following to keep track of trust funds?
   a. a columnar system

119

b. a reconciliation system

c. a system deemed compatible with accepted accounting practices

d. either a or c

67. When doing her inspection of Bob's house, agent Jane notices a few water stains on the upstairs bedroom ceiling. When asked, Bob says, "The roof leaks, but only if it rains hard." This is an example of
a. a material fact
b. something that Jane should hold in confidence because she represents Bob
c. something that should be painted over so that it no longer shows
d. both b and c

68. A Realtor® is
a. a member of the N.A.R.
b. anyone licensed by the Bureau of Real Estate
c. any valid real estate brokerage
d. none of the above

69. Sally and Janet are the only two brokers in a small town where the commercial district is primarily on the north side of town and the residential district is primarily on the south side of town. Sally and Janet agree that to better serve their clients, Sally would take listings only on the commercial north side of town while Janet would take listings only on the south side of town. This is an example of
a. tying arrangement
b. commingling
c. group boycott
d. none of the above

70. A broker-principal relationship usually is created by a
a. deposit receipt
b. listing agreement
c. purchase agreement
d. none of the above

71. Julie is a salesperson who receives 40% of the commission on all sales that her employing broker, Susan, receives due to Julie's effort. Julie receives a commission of $9,350 due to her procurement of the sale of a house for which Susan had a 5% commission listing agreement. How much did the house sell for?
    a. $187,000
    b. $467,500
    c. $233,750
    d. $311,667

72. After owning a building for nine years, Kevin sold it for $1,750,000. His initial cost for the building was $2,150,000. What was the average annual rate of depreciation (loss in value) of the building?
    a. 2.07%
    b. 2.54%
    c. 2.33%
    d. 2.86%

73. Sam is a salesperson who receives 50% of the commission on all sales commissions that his employing broker, Bob, receives due to Sam's effort. Sam receives a commission of $8,450 due to his procurement of the sale of a house for which Bob had a 6% commission listing agreement. How much did the house sell for?
    a. $140,833
    b. $422,500
    c. $280,000
    d. none of the above

74. Susan owns a 2-acre rectangular lot and wishes to divide it into 4 lots of equal size, each having a depth of 200 feet. What would be the width of each of these lots?
    a. 108.9 feet
    b. 217.8 feet
    c. 54.45 feet
    d. none of the above

75. A building depreciates by 2% each year. How many years will it take for the building to be worth only 70% of its initial value?
    a. 20 years
    b. 18 years
    c. 16 years
    d. none of the above

76. A mortgage that typically allows borrowers to borrow only what they need as they need it is
   a. a standby mortgage
   b. a blanket mortgage
   c. a purchase money mortgage
   d. home equity mortgage

77. The borrower has how long after a sheriff's sale in which to redeem the property if the lender pursues a deficiency judgment?
   a. 3 months
   b. 6 months
   c. 1 year
   d. there is no redemption period after a sheriff's sale is completed

78. Periodic payments that consist of interest only is a characteristic of
   a. a bridge loan
   b. a fully amortized loan
   c. a straight note
   d. an installment note

79. A negative amortized loan is
   a. a promissory note in which periodic payments are made, usually consisting of interest due and some repayment of principal
   b. a loan by which the installment payments do not cover all of the interest due — the unpaid part of the interest due being tacked onto the principal, thereby causing the principal to grow as each month goes by
   c. a security instrument for a loan for homeowners over the age of 62 who have a large amount of equity in their homes, usually designed to provide such homeowners with monthly payments, often over the lifetime of the last surviving homeowner who either moves out of the house or dies
   d. a loan under which payments are sufficient to pay off the entire loan by the end of the loan term

80. The clause in a deed of trust that permits the trustee to sell the property if the borrower defaults is
   a. an alienation clause
   b. an assumption clause
   c. a due-on-sale clause
   d. power of sale clause

81. Within how many days after receiving a request for reconveyance must the trustee execute and record a deed of reconveyance?
    a. 21 days
    b. 30 days
    c. 45 days
    d. 60 days

82. A defeasance clause states that
    a. the mortgage or deed of trust will have a lower priority than a mortgage or deed of trust recorded later
    b. when the loan is paid in full, the lender must release its lien from the property
    c. if the property is sold, the balance of the loan is due and payable immediately
    d. none of the above

83. A junior mortgage is a
    a. first mortgage
    b. mortgage that, relative to another mortgage, has a lower loan balance
    c. nonconforming mortgage
    d. none of the above

84. An instrument used to eliminate a deed of trust from the records is
    a. a certificate of completion
    b. an assumption upon completion
    c. a certificate of discharge
    d. none of the above

85. An installment payment that is significantly greater than prior payments is referred to as
    a. a bridge payment
    b. an adjustment payment
    c. a balloon payment
    d. none of the above

86. Conventional mortgages are

a. FHA insured
b. VA guaranteed
c. both a and b
d. neither a nor b

87. The SAFE Act requires how many hours of pre-license education for state-licensed MLOs?
a. 10
b. 15
c. 20
d. 25

88. Life insurance companies operating in the primary mortgage market primarily fund
a. residential loans
b. REIT loans
c. loans for commercial and industrial properties
d. FHA loans

89. If it qualifies, one of the advantages of a REIT is
a. that it only needs 10 persons to get started
b. that it only needs 50 persons to get started
c. pass-through of corporate income
d. none of the above

90. Which of the following terms least belongs with the others?
a. tax returns for self-employed persons
b. FICO scores
c. eligibility to receive pension or Social Security income for retired persons
d. W-2 statements for wage earners

91. FHA loans are
a. assumable
b. assumable with FHA approval
c. never assumable
d. none of the above

92. VA loans are
a. assumable
b. assumable with VA approval

c. never assumable

d. none of the above

93. CalVet loans are used to finance the purchase of
   a. farms
   b. residences
   c. commercial buildings
   d. both a and b

94. Loans that exceed certain designated limits are referred to as
   a. conforming loans
   b. excessive loans
   c. jumbo loans
   d. FHA-insured loans

95. Portfolio loans are
   a. loans retained by primary lenders
   b. loans purchased by Fannie Mae
   c. loans purchased by Freddie Mac
   d. referred to as mortgage-backed securities

96. The four elements of value are
   a. utility, scarcity, demand, conformity
   b. conformity, transferability, demand, utility
   c. utility, scarcity, demand, highest and best use
   d. utility, scarcity, demand, transferability

97. A real estate appraisal
   a. determines market price
   b. determines market value
   c. estimates market value
   d. guarantees a minimum market value

98. The scope of practice of a Trainee License is
   a. any property that the supervising appraiser is permitted to appraise up to a transaction value of $250,000
   b. any property that the supervising appraiser is permitted to appraise up to a transaction value of $500,000

   c. any property that the supervising appraiser is permitted to appraise up to a transaction value of $1 million

   d. any property that the supervising appraiser is permitted to appraise

99. A property rents for $3,000 per month and has additional income from parking fees of $200 per month. What is the value of the property as calculated using a monthly gross rent multiplier of 140 if the property has $150 per month upkeep expenses?
   a. $448,000
   b. $399,000
   c. $427,000
   d. $420,000

100. What was the original price of a condo if five years after its purchase it has depreciated by 3% and its current value is $250,000?
   a. $242,500
   b. $242,718
   c. $257,732
   d. $294,118

101. Which of the following terms least belongs with the others?
   a. transferability
   b. conformity
   c. utility
   d. demand

102. The assessed value of a property is usually its
   a. market price
   b. subjective value
   c. market value
   d. replacement cost

103. The scope of permitted practice of a Certified Residential License is
   a. any non-complex 1-4 unit residential property with a transaction value up to $1 million; and non-residential property with a transaction value up to $250,000
   b. any 1-4 unit residential property without regard to transaction value or complexity; and non-residential property with a transaction value up to $500,000

c. all real estate without regard to transaction value or complexity

d. none of the above

104. A property rents for $2,000 per month. What would be the value of the property as calculated using a monthly gross income multiplier of 150 if the property also obtained income of $100 per month from parking fees?
a. $300,000
b. $315,000
c. $285,000
d. none of the above

105. A decrease in land values would likely result from
a. scarcity
b. book depreciation
c. functional obsolescence
d. lack of demand

106. The delivery to escrow of deposits and transfer instruments
a. must occur before closing
b. may occur after closing
c. must be irrevocable
d. both a and c

107. If a real estate broker advertises that he or she serves as an escrow agent, the broker must state that
a. such services are only in connection with real estate transactions in which the broker is involved
b. such services are available for any real estate transaction regardless of the ethnicity of the parties
c. such services are available for any real estate transaction regardless of the religion of the parties
d. all of the above

108. Ways in which an escrow can terminate include
a. closing
b. default
c. issuance of a preliminary title report
d. either a or b

109. The California Financial Code provides that, unless exempted, an escrow agent
    a. must be a corporation
    b. must be licensed by the Bureau of Real Estate
    c. must be a party to the real estate transaction
    d. both a and b

110. The proper delivery to escrow of deposits and transfer instruments
    a. can be revoked by either party within three days of delivery
    b. can be revoked by either party within two days of delivery
    c. can be revoked by either party within one day of delivery
    d. none of the above

111. Closing acts performed by the escrow agent include
    a. recording the deed and the deed of trust at the recorder's office, confirming the recordation, and informing the principles of the recordation
    b. delivering or mailing the settlement statement to the borrower and the seller
    c. verifying that the title policy is in place and sending the original policy to the borrower
    d. all of the above

112. A 1099-S report is
    a. required by California law for all sales of California real estate
    b. a settlement statement required by HUD for certain real estate transactions
    c. only required if the seller is a non-resident alien
    d. none of the above

113. Loan servicing is
    a. the administration of escrow involving the deposit of transfer instruments and purchase money for a real estate transaction
    b. the withholding of a certain amount realized from the sale of real property and sending that amount the IRS
    c. the administration of a loan from the time the loan proceeds are dispersed to the time the loan is paid off in full
    d. none of the above

114. If a real estate transaction involves a seller who is a non-resident alien
    a. the seller has the responsibility to determine whether the buyer is a non-resident alien; and if so, the seller has the responsibility of

withholding 10% of the amount realized from the sale and sending that 10% of the IRS

b. the lender has the responsibility to determine whether the seller is a non-resident alien; and if so, the lender has the responsibility of withholding 10% of the amount realized from the sale and sending that 10% of the IRS

c. the buyer has the responsibility to determine whether the seller is a non-resident alien; and if so, the buyer has the responsibility of withholding 10% of the amount realized from the sale and sending that 10% of the IRS

d. none of the above

115. For some real estate transactions, FIRPTA requires the withholding of what percentage of the amount realized from the sale?
a. 3⅓
b. 5
c. 10
d. none of the above

116. The screening fee that a landlord may charge an applicant for residential property
a. may be increased by no more than 5% per year
b. may be increased by no more than 3% per year
c. may be increased by no more than 2% per year
d. may be increased commensurate with the Consumer Price Index

117. If utilities are separately metered and are put in the tenant's name, and if the tenant vacates the premises without paying for the utilities, the utilities provider may charge
a. the landlord for the unpaid utilities bill
b. the next tenant who leases the premises for the unpaid utilities bill
c. neither a nor b
d. either a or b

118. Compared to the period for notice of termination of a rental in a mobile home park, the period for notice of termination of a single-family home in general is
a. shorter
b. longer
c. the same
d. none of the above

119. For a residential building, California law requires that the landlord

a. provide effective waterproofing and weather protection of the roof
b. install and maintain plumbing and gas facilities that conform to applicable law
c. provide and maintain heating facilities that conform to applicable law
d. all of the above

120. A legal doctrine that states that there is a legally enforceable relationship between persons who are parties to a contract is
a. an implied warranty that the premises are suitable for human habitation
b. novation
c. privity of estate
d. privity of contract

121. A screening fee charged to an applicant for a residential property
a. may be for the actual costs of such items as credit reports and verification of references
b. may be for any reasonable amount
c. may not exceed $75
d. none of the above

122. In a residential lease, the landlord is responsible for providing the availability of basic utilities
a. and is responsible for paying these utilities unless the lease specifically provides otherwise
b. but is never responsible for paying for the utilities
c. but is not obligated to pay for the utilities unless so specified in the lease
d. none of the above

123. Absent a tax treaty that provides for a lower rate, under FIRPTA a renter who makes payments to a non-resident alien must withhold a flat rate of what part of the rents?
a. 10%
b. 20%
c. 30%
d. none of the above

124. Absent relevant provisions in a non-residential lease, the landlord has no legal duty to
    a. make repairs
    b. provide the premises in a condition suitable for the tenant's purposes
    c. both a and b
    d. neither a nor b

125. Privity of contract is
    a. a legal doctrine that states that a legally enforceable relationship exists between the persons who are parties to a contract
    b. a legal doctrine that states that a legally enforceable relationship exists between the parties who hold interests in the same real property
    c. both a and b
    d. neither a nor b

126. The refusal to loan in particular areas is called
    a. steering
    b. blockbusting
    c. variance
    d. redlining

127. An R-1 zone likely refers to a
    a. zoning category for condominiums and apartment buildings
    b. zoning category for commercial activities
    c. zoning category for light industrial activities
    d. zoning category for single-family homes

128. A final public report is required by the
    a. Subdivision Map Act
    b. Unruh Civil Rights Act
    c. Holden Act
    d. Subdivided Lands Law

129. The term of a preliminary public report for a subdivision is
    a. 2 years and may not be extended through renewal
    b. 2 years and may be extended through renewal
    c. 5 years and may be extended through renewal
    d. 1 year and may be extended through renewal

130. The Civil Rights Act of 1968 and its 1974 and 1988 amendments prohibit
    a. discriminatory advertising in the housing market
    b. discriminatory access to multiple listing services
    c. both a and b
    d. neither a nor b

131. Directing protected classes away from, or toward, particular areas is called
    a. steering
    b. redlining
    c. blockbusting
    d. none of the above

132. A zoning exception for areas that are zoned for the first time or that are rezoned where established property uses that previously were permitted do not conform to new zoning requirements is called a
    a. re-zoning amendment
    b. variance
    c. conditional use
    d. none of the above

133. The Subdivision Map Act requires tentative maps for subdivisions that create how many parcels?
    a. 5 or more
    b. 4 or more
    c. 3 or more
    d. 2 or more

134. If a subdivision undergoes "material change" after the issuance of a final public report, the subdivider must
    a. apply for a new preliminary public report
    b. re-apply for a new final public report
    c. apply for a conditional use report
    d. none of the above

135. Federal law provides an exception to the prohibition of discrimination based on familial status to allow children to be excluded from properties

a. where at least 70% of the dwelling units are occupied by persons 55 years of age or older

b. where all dwelling units are less than 500 ft.² in size

c. where at least 70% of the dwelling units are occupied by at least one person who is over 62 years of age

d. none of the above

136. An apartment building worth $5 million is traded in a 1031 exchange for another apartment building worth $5 million plus $100,000 cash. How much will the original owner of the $5 million apartment building recognize as taxable income due to the exchange at the time of the exchange?

a. $0

b. $100,000

c. he or she will recognize a loss of $100,000

d. $5,100,000 less the home's depreciated basis

137. The California county documentary transfer tax rate is

a. $1.10 per $500 or fraction thereof

b. $0.55 per $500 or fraction thereof

c. $1.00 per $1,000 or fraction thereof

d. $1.00 per $500 or fraction thereof

138. Proposition 58

a. can be used to reduce the assessed value of property in times of decreasing property values

b. provides for an exclusion from reassessment for certain transfers from grandparents to their grandchildren, but not transfers from grandchildren to their grandparents

c. allows certain older persons to transfer the adjusted basis of their present principal residence to a replacement if the replacement is in the same county and is of equal or lesser value than the prior residence

d. provides for an exclusion from reassessment when property is transferred between spouses

139. Income tax benefits of home ownership include

a. under certain circumstances mortgage interest paid on a second home is deductible

b. up to a certain limit, mortgage interest on a primary residence can be deducted

c. both a and b

d. neither a nor b

140. A homeowner's exclusion from capital gains on the sale of a personal residence can be taken
    a. only once
    b. once every two years
    c. only if the homeowner had lived in the residence for five consecutive years
    d. only if the homeowner had lived in the residence for 3 out of the last 5 years

141. In a 1031 exchange, cash and/or unlike property received is referred to as
    a. like-kind of property
    b. tax-deferred property
    c. passive income
    d. none of the above

142. The veteran's exemption provides an exemption of up to how much from the assessed value of a qualified veteran's property?
    a. $4,000
    b. $7,000
    c. $10,000
    d. $15,000

143. Proposition 8
    a. can reduce the assessed value of property in times of decreasing property values
    b. provides for an exclusion from reassessment when the property is transferred between spouses
    c. provides for an exclusion from reassessment for certain transfers from grandparents to grandchildren
    d. none of the above

144. Income tax benefits of home ownership include

a. repairs and maintenance of a taxpayer's personal residence are tax deductible

b. loss on the sale of a taxpayer's personal residence is tax deductible

c. both a and b

d. neither a nor b

145. Alice and Bob, who have been married for five years and have lived in the same personal residence for the past four years, have just sold their condo. If a file a joint return, they may exclude how much from capital gains on the sale?

a. $0

b. $150,000

c. $250,000

d. none of the above

146. A conduit is

a. the space between the ground and the first floor that permits access beneath the building

b. a channel in a chimney through which flames and smoke pass upward to the outer air

c. a beam connecting pairs of opposite rafters

d. a pipe in which electrical wiring is installed

147. A crawlspace is

a. a channel in a chimney through which flame and smoke passes upward to the outer air

b. the space between the ground and the first floor that permits access beneath the building

c. a metal pipe in which electrical wiring is installed

d. the overhang of a roof that projects over an exterior wall of a house

148. One of a series of parallel heavy horizontal timbers used to support floor or ceiling loads is a

a. joist

b. rafter

c. stud

d. ridgeboard

149. As that term is defined in the California Health and Safety Code, a manufactured home would be
    a. constructed before June 15, 1976
    b. constructed on or after June 15, 1976
    c. both a and b
    d. neither a nor b

150. A manufactured home is considered real property when
    a. it is affixed to a permanent foundation
    b. it is registered with the CalBRE
    c. both a and b
    d. neither a nor b

Answers to Practice Exam #2

Note: If you would like to obtain a deeper understanding of the real estate principles behind the following answers, consult the textbook *California Real Estate Principles and License Preparation, 2nd Edition*, which is available both in print and Kindle formats on Amazon.com. The author, Jim Bainbridge, is a graduate of Harvard Law School, a member of the California Bar, and a licensed California real estate broker.

1. a. An easement created by express grant or by express reservation cannot be terminated by nonuse.

2. d. Things attached to the land by roots and things embedded in the land both constitute real property.

3. c. Growing crops that are produced through a tenant farmer's labor are called emblements, and a prescriptive easement can be terminated by a period of five years of nonuse.

4. b. Answer a relates to whether an encroachment was made by a good-faith improver.

5. a. The support that soil receives from the land adjacent to it is called lateral support.

6. a. In order for an easement in gross to exist, there must be a servient tenement but not a dominant tenement.

7. c. A deed restriction would be created by the grantor of the deed.

8. d. An estate at will, a tenancy at sufferance, and an estate for years are all nonfreehold estates.

9. d. "Bundle of rights" refers to rights or interests in land that may include possession, the right to exclude others, and the right to encumber the property.

10. a. A prescriptive easement can arise if someone uses property without permission for at least five years.

11. b. A life tenant is obligated to act reasonably to avoid harming ("wasting") the value of the future interest of the property.

12. a. An estate from period to period, an estate at will, and an estate for years, are all leasehold estates.

13.   b. The important differences between a lease and a license are that the lessee has the exclusive right to possession of the property (the licensee only has the non-exclusive right to use) and the lessee has a statutory right to be given written notice that his or her rights in the property are being revoked (the licensee does not).

14.   c. A license is not considered an estate; it does not run with the land. If ownership of the property that the licensee has permission to use is transferred, the license is revoked.

15.   c. A license to use is a personal right to use property on a nonexclusive basis.

16.   d. If Susan dies before Joe, an estate in which Susan granted to Joe an estate for his life would continue for the duration of Joe's life.

17.   d. A freehold estate is also known as an estate of inheritance.

18.   c. A has a reversionary interest in the property, which will revert to A upon C's death.

19.   b. A leasehold estate is a less-than-freehold estate.

20.   d. A fee simple defeasible, a lease, and a fee simple absolute are all estates

21.   b. The possession must be continuous and uninterrupted for 5 years.

22.   c. To acquire a prescriptive easement, the possession or use must be hostile and there must be a claim of right or color of title.

23.   c. Foreclosure sale, partition action, and sheriff's sale are ways in which private persons can acquire title to real property.

24.   c. Eminent domain is not an exercise of police power. Also, property acquired through eminent domain must be paid for by the condemning authority.

25.   a. Most individuals acquire or transfer title to real property by means of a grant deed.

26.   a. An acre = 43,560 ft.^{2}

27.   d. Escheat is a process whereby property passes to the state if a person owning the property dies intestate without heirs.

28.   d. A warranty deed is a deed in which the grantor warrants that the title being conveyed is good and free from defects or encumbrances, and that the grantor will defend the title against all suits. It also conveys after-acquired interests.

29. a. A sheriff's deed is the type of deed given to the purchaser after a sheriff's sale.

30. d. If a broker is involved in the probate sale of a decedent's estate property, the broker will likely receive whatever commission the court approves.

31. c. Both property inherited during marriage and rents from separately owned property are separate property (unless the rent is generated in significant part from the labor of one of the spouses).

32. b. Gifts purchased with community property, such as birthday or anniversary gifts, are considered the separate property of the spouse who receives the gifts.

33. c. Regarding community property, both spouses must agree in writing to all transfers of, or encumbrances on, community real property or on the furniture or furnishings of the family home.

34. a. A deed that conveys property as community property with right of survivorship must be signed by the grantees.

35. c. When a partner dies, title to the property rests entirely in the surviving partners and the decedent's estate or heirs acquire no direct interest in the property of the partnership or in its management. The decedent's estate or heirs do, however, have a right to an accounting and a share of the partnership profits and value upon dissolution.

36. b. Wages earned during marriage become community property.

37. d. A corporation may not hold title in real property as a joint tenant because the corporation has no natural life span, thus destroying any notion of right of survivorship.

38. b. Without contrary evidence, married couples and registered domestic partners are presumed to hold title in property as community property.

39. a. Without contrary evidence, property held by persons who are not married and are not registered domestic partners is presumed to be held by those persons as tenants in common.

40. d. Both tenancy in common and community property are subject to disposition by will.

41. b. A notice of cessation may be recorded by the owner if there has been a continuous cessation of labor on the work of improvement for at least 30 days prior to the recordation.

42. c. The holder of a mechanics lien must file a foreclosure action within 90 days after recordation of the lien. A notice of completion must be recorded within 15 days of the completion of a work of improvement.

43. b. Answer a is incorrect because the notice referred to is a notice of nonresponsibility.

44. c. All mechanics liens relating to the same work of improvement have equal priority, and each mechanics lien holder is entitled to collect his or her pro rata (proportional) share of the work furnished.

45. c. The amount of protection California homestead law provides is $75,000 for an individual and $175,000 if the homeowner is 55 years of age or older and single with an annual income of $15,000 or less, and the sale is an *involuntary* sale.

46. d. If the owner does not file a notice of completion or a notice of cessation, a subcontractor has 90 days in which to file a mechanics lien.

47. b. A direct contractor has 20 days after first providing labor or material to a work of improvement to serve a preliminary notice on a construction lender.

48. a. A subcontractor has 20 days after first providing the labor or material to a work of improvement to file a preliminary notice.

49. c. In a lawsuit involving real property, a lis pendens may issue during the pendency of the action, followed by a judgment lien and writ of execution.

50. d. A wage earner does not need to file a preliminary notice to qualify for mechanics lien.

51. a. An offeree can reject, not revoke, the offer.

52. d. For a contract to be valid, both its consideration and its object must be lawful. If a contract has only one object and that object is unlawful, the entire contract is void. However, if the contract has several objects, some of which are valid, the contract would normally be valid and enforced as to the lawful objects only.

53. b. While consideration can be a forbearance, consideration need not be of essentially equal value to what is given in exchange for the consideration.

54. c. The California Statute of Frauds provides that certain contracts are invalid, unless they, or some note or memorandum thereof, are in writing and subscribed by the party to be charged or by the party's agent. Contracts that are covered by the Statute of Frauds and that fail to be in writing are not void but are unenforceable.

55. c. Both of the agreements stated in answers a and b must be in writing to satisfy the statute of frauds.

56.   d. A valid contract need not be in writing but must have a lawful object and the parties must be capable of contracting.

57.   c. Unless Joe receives an acceptance from Janet before the expiration of his offer, he may revoke his offer at any time.

58.   d. A counter offer by an offeree terminates the original offeror's offer and presents an offer to the original offeror.

59.   d. Neither parole evidence nor a writing evidencing a contract is necessary to form a valid contract.

60.   b. An exclusive agency listing is an agreement that gives a broker the right to sell property and receive compensation (usually a commission) if the property is sold by anyone other than the owner of the property during the term of the listing.

61.   b. A post-dated check is not a promissory note, a negotiable instrument, or a cash equivalent — it is merely a promise to pay.

62.   a. The account must be designated in the broker's name as trustee and must be maintained in an account insured by the FDIC.

63.   a. The broker must, within *25 days* of receiving a commission into the trust account, withdraw the amount of the commission from the account.

64.   d. After the acceptance of an offer, the check may be given to the seller only if the seller and the buyer expressly so provide in writing, and no part of the deposit may be refunded by an agent or a subagent of the seller without the express written permission of the seller.

65.   d. Sally should file an interpleader, give the deposit to the clerk of the court, and let her client and the buyer have at it.

66.   d. A broker may use a columnar system or a system deemed compatible with accepted accounting practices to keep track of trust funds.

67.   a. A leaking roof is a material fact that must be disclosed to any potential buyer by both the seller and the agent.

68.   a. A Realtor® is a member of the National Association of Realtors® (the N.A.R.). Real estate agents need not become a member of the N.A.R.

69.   d. This is an example of illegal market allocation.

70.   b. A broker-principal relationship usually is created by a listing agreement.

71.   b. Julie effectively receives 2% of the sales she makes from Susan's listing. Therefore, $9,350 = 2% of Sales Price. $9,350 ÷ .02 = $467,500.

72. a. Loss = $2,150,000 $-1,750,000 = $400,000.
Average annual loss = $400,000 ÷ 9 years = $44,444.4444/yr.
$44,444.4444/yr. ÷ $2,150,000 = 2.07% per year.

73. d. Sam effectively receives 3% of the sales he makes from Bob's listing. (Note that there would be no cooperating agent involved in such cases this.) Therefore, $8,450 = 3% of Sales Price.
$8,450 ÷ .03 = $281,667.

74. a. Susan's 2-acre lot has 2 x 43,560 ft.² = 87,120 ft.². Therefore, each of the equal-size lots would be 87,120 ft.² ÷ 4 = 21,780 ft.². 21,700 ft.² ÷ 200 ft. = 108.9 ft. width.

75. d. The answer can be rephrased as: How long does it take to depreciate by 30%. Since the building depreciates 2%/yr., it takes 30% ÷ 2%/yr. = 15 years.

76. d. A mortgage that typically allows borrowers to borrow only what they need as they need it is a home equity mortgage.

77. c. If the lender elects to pursue a deficiency judgment, the borrower has one year to redeem the property.

78. c. A straight note is a promissory note in which periodic payments consist of interest only.

79. b. A negative amortized loan is a loan by which the installment payments do not cover all of the interest due — the unpaid part of the interest due being tacked onto the principal, thereby causing the principal to grow as each month goes by.

80. d. The clause in a deed of trust that permits the trustee to sell the property if the borrower defaults is the power-of-sale clause.

81. a. After receiving a request for reconveyance, the trustee must within 21 days execute and record a deed of reconveyance.

82. b. A defeasance clause is a provision in a loan that states that when the loan debt has been fully paid, the lender must release the property from the lien so that legal title free from the lien will be owned by the borrower.

83. d. A junior mortgage is a mortgage that, relative to another mortgage, has a lower lien-priority position.

84. d. A deed of reconveyance is an instrument signed by the trustee of a deed of trust that eliminates the deed of trust lien from the records and conveys the legal title to the borrower.

85. c. A balloon payment is a payment, usually the final payment, of an installment loan that is significantly greater than prior payments —

"significantly greater" generally considered as being more than twice the lowest installment payment paid over the loan term.

86.   d. A conventional mortgage is a mortgage that is not FHA insured or VA guaranteed.

87.   c. The SAFE Act requires 20 hours of pre-license education for state-licensed MLOs.

88.   c. While institutional lenders such as state banks, national banks, and savings and loans create many residential loans, life insurance companies operating in the primary mortgage market create mortgages mainly for large commercial and industrial properties.

89.   c. If it is able to satisfy certain criteria, a REIT may pass-through income for U.S. corporate tax purposes.

90.   b. W-2 statements for wage earners, tax returns for self-employed persons, and eligibility to receive pension or Social Security income for retired persons are considered components of a potential borrower's capacity to repay a loan.

91.   b. FHA loans are assumable with FHA approval.

92.   b. VA loans are assumable with VA approval.

93.   d. CalVet loans can be used to finance the purchase of farms and residences.

94.   c. A jumbo loan is a loan the amount of which exceeds conforming loan limits set by the FHFA on an annual basis.

95.   a. Portfolio loans are loans that primary lenders retain in their own investment portfolios rather than sell into the secondary market.

96.   d. The four elements of value are utility, scarcity, demand, transferability.

97.   c. An appraisal does not determine or guarantee any value or price — it is an estimate based on an expert evaluation by an appraiser.

98.   d. The scope of practice of a Trainee License is any property that the supervising appraiser is permitted to appraise.

99.   d. $3,000 x 140 = $420,000. Using the gross rent multiplier, neither expenses nor additional income are included in the calculation.

100. c. $250,000 ÷ .97 = $257,732.

101. b. The four elements of value are transferability, utility, scarcity, and demand.

102. c. The most common purpose of an appraisal is to estimate the market value of a property.

103. d. The scope of a Certified Residential License is any 1-4 unit residential property without regard to transaction value or complexity; and non-residential property with a transaction value up to $250,000.

104. b. GIM considers all income, not just rents, in calculating value.

105. d. Neither book depreciation nor functional obsolescence applies to land. Scarcity would tend to increase the value of land, not decrease it.

106. d. The delivery to escrow of the deposits and transfer instruments must be irrevocable and, of course, must occur during the escrow.

107. a. A broker may not state in any advertisement that he or she serves as an escrow agent without specifying that such services are only in connection with real estate transactions in which the broker is involved.

108. d. There are three ways in which an escrow can terminate: closing, mutual agreement, or default.

109. a. The California Financial Code provides that, unless exempted, an escrow agent must be a corporation.

110. d. The proper delivery to escrow of the deposits and transfer instruments must be irrevocable.

111. d. Closing acts performed by the escrow agent include (1) recording the deed and the deed of trust at the recorder's office, confirming the recordation, and informing the principles of the recordation; (2) delivering or mailing the settlement statement to the borrower and seller; (3) delivering all of the deposits and funds allocated pursuant to the settlement statement; and (4) verifying that the title policy is in place and sending the original policy to the borrower.

112. d. A 1099-S report is a report required by *federal* law to be submitted on IRS Form 1099-S by escrow agents to report the sale of real estate, giving the seller's name, Social Security number, and the gross sale proceeds.

113. c. Loan servicing is the administration of a loan from the time the loan proceeds are dispersed to the time the loan is paid off in full.

114. c. FIRPTA states that, with certain exceptions, the buyer must determine whether the seller is a nonresident alien; and if so, the buyer has the responsibility of withholding 10% of the amount realized from the sale and sending that 10% of the IRS.

115. c. Foreign Investment in Real Property Tax Act (FIRPTA) is a federal act that, with certain exceptions, requires the buyer in a real estate

transaction to determine whether the seller is a non-resident alien; and if so, the buyer has the responsibility of withholding 10% of the amount realized from the sale and sending that 10% of the IRS.

116. d. The screening fee that a landlord may charge an applicant for a residential property may be increased commensurate with the Consumer Price Index.

117. c. If utilities are separately metered, the tenant is generally responsible for putting the utilities in the tenant's name, in which case the utilities provider may not charge either the property owner or future tenants for unpaid utility bills.

118. a. The applicable notice period for a single-family is 30 days (unless the tenant has lived in the premises for a year or more, in which case the notice period is 60 days), while the notice period for a rental in a mobile home park is 60 days.

119. d. For a residential building, California law requires the landlord to do all of the things itemized in answers a, b, and c.

120. d. Privity of contract is a legal doctrine that states that a legally enforceable relationship exists between the persons who are parties to a contract.

121. d. The screening fee cannot be more than the landlord's actual costs and may not exceed a certain specified amount, which started at $30 and may be increased commensurate with the Consumer Price Index beginning on January 1, 1998.

122. c. In a residential lease, the landlord is responsible for providing the availability of basic utilities but is not obligated to pay for the utilities unless so specified in the lease.

123. c. Under FIRPTA, a renter who makes rent payments to a non-resident alien must withhold a flat rate of 30% of the rents, unless a tax treaty provides for a lower rate.

124. c. Absent relevant provisions in a non-residential lease, the landlord has no legal duty to make repairs or to provide the premises in a condition suitable for the tenant's intended purpose; except that (1) the landlord must maintain and repair those parts of the premises for which the landlord has contractually assumed such obligation pursuant to the terms of the lease, and (2) the landlord must ensure that building codes and other government ordinances are satisfied if the tenant has not assumed those obligations in the lease.

125. a. Privity of contract is a legal doctrine that states that a legally enforceable relationship exists between the persons who are parties to a contract.

126. d. Redlining is the illegal practice of refusing to make loans for real property in particular areas.

127. d. An R-1 zone likely refers to a zone for single-family homes.

128. d. A final public report is required by the Subdivided Lands Law.

129. d. The term of a preliminary public report for subdivision is 1 year and may be extended through renewal.

130. c. The Civil Rights Act of 1968 and its 1974 and 1988 amendments prohibit numerous discriminatory acts, including discriminatory advertising in the housing market and discriminatory access to multiple listing services.

131. a. Steering is the illegal practice of directing people of protected classes away from, or toward, housing in particular areas.

132. d. A zoning exception for areas that are zoned for the first time or that are rezoned where established property uses that previously were permitted do not conform to new zoning requirements is called a nonconforming use.

133. a. With certain exceptions, the Subdivision Map Act requires tentative and final maps for subdivisions that create 5 or more parcels, 5 or more condominiums, a community apartment project containing 5 or more interests, or the conversion of a dwelling into a stock cooperative of 5 or more dwelling units.

134. d. If a subdivision undergoes "material change" after the issuance of a final public report, the subdivider must apply for an amended public report.

135. d. Federal law provides an exception to the prohibition of discrimination based on familial status to allow children to be excluded from properties (1) occupied solely by persons 62 years of age or older; or (2) where at least 80% of the dwelling units are occupied by at least one person who is 55 years of age or older.

136. b. Cash and/or unlike property received in a 1031 exchange is recognized as taxable income from the exchange at the time of the exchange.

137. b. The California county documentary transfer tax rate is $0.55 per $500 or fraction thereof.

138. d. Proposition 58 provides for an exclusion from reassessment when property is transferred between spouses. It also provides for an exclusion from reassessment of a transfer of a principal residence and transfers of the first $1 million of other real property between parent and child.

139. c. Interest paid on a mortgage secured by a principal residence or by a second home is deductible from personal income. There is a limit on how much interest can be deducted, which limit currently is the interest on the portion of a loan that does not exceed $1 million. The mortgage interest deduction can only be taken on a principal residence and one second home.

140. b. The homeowner's exclusion can only be taken once every two years.

141. d. In a 1031 exchange, cash and/or unlike property received is referred to as boot.

142. a. The veteran's exemption provides an exemption of up to $4,000 from the assessed value of a qualified veteran's property.

143. a. Proposition 8 requires the county assessor to assess real property either at the property's Proposition 13 adjusted value or its current market value, whichever is less. Proposition 8 can, therefore, reduce the assessed value of property in times of decreasing property values.

144. d. Compared to ownership of investment properties, there are a few negative tax consequences of home ownership. For example, loss on the sale of a taxpayer's personal residence is not tax deductible. Repairs, maintenance, and other operating expenses of owning a principal place of residence are also not tax deductible.

145. d. They may exclude $500,000 from the capital gains on the sale.

146. d. A conduit is a pipe in which electrical wiring is installed.

147. b. A crawlspace is the space between the ground and first floor that permits access beneath the building.

148. a. A joist is one of a series of parallel heavy horizontal timbers used to support floor or ceiling loads.

149. b. As defined in a California Health and Safety Code, a manufactured home is constructed on or after June 15, 1976.

150. a. A manufactured home is considered real estate when it is affixed to a permanent foundation. A manufactured home is registered with the Department of Housing and Community Development, not the CalBRE.

Practice Exam #3:

1. In 1850
   a. California became a state
   b. the Treaty of Guadalupe Hidalgo was signed
   c. both a and b
   d. neither a nor b

2. The "bundle of rights" associated with property includes the right to
   a. encumber
   b. sell
   c. both a and b
   d. neither a nor b

3. Real property includes
   a. appurtenances
   b. land
   c. both a and b
   d. neither a nor b

4. Which of the following least belongs with the others?
   a. emblements
   b. support rights
   c. stock in a mutual water company
   d. an easement appurtenant

5. The law of capture is associated with
   a. oil
   b. geothermal steam
   c. gas
   d. all of the above

6. A developer in city X is preparing a parcel of land Y for residential development. A commercial acre in Y probably contains
   a. 43,650 square feet
   b. 43,560 square feet
   c. less than 43,560 square feet
   d. between 43,650 and 43,560 square feet

7. Crops on leased land

a. are always real property
b. are always personal property
c. are always owned by the tenant farmer
d. may be either personal or real property, depending on the lease terms

8. Trade fixtures
    a. generally can be removed if the removal does not cause irreparable harm
    b. generally cannot be removed without the landlord's consent
    c. occur only in certain lease situations
    d. both a and c

9. The legal right to all of the gas, oil, and steam produced from wells drilled directly underneath a landowner's property is called
    a. a bundle of rights
    b. the law of capture
    c. the law of underground liquids
    d. the law emblements

10. The property burdened by an easement is called
    a. a servient tenement
    b. a dominant tenement
    c. an encroachment
    d. a lateral support

11. A mortgage is
    a. an estate
    b. a freehold estate
    c. a fee simple defeasible estate
    d. not considered an estate

12. Which of the following is (are) false?
    a. an estate for years is a periodic tenancy
    b. an easement that benefits not land but a legal person is called an easement in gross
    c. an estate at will can be terminated by the landlord's giving a 30-day notice
    d. none of the above

13. The degree, quantity, nature, duration, and interest one has in real property is referred to as
    a. a remainder
    b. a reversion
    c. a license

d. an estate

14. Zoning codes and building restrictions are examples of
   a. governmental use of police power
   b. conditions subsequent
   c. both a and b
   d. neither a nor b

15. When property is transferred, the law presumes that
   a. a nonfreehold estate is being transferred
   b. a fee simple absolute is being transferred
   c. a leasehold estate is being transferred
   d. the title is subject to a condition subsequent

16. The term of a lease for agricultural land cannot exceed
   a. 89 years
   b. 75 years
   c. 51 years
   d. none of the above

17. The term of the lease for a city lot cannot exceed
   a. 49 years
   b. 51 years
   c. 89 years
   d. none of the above

18. A reversionary interest in real property often refers to
   a. a remainderman
   b. life estates
   c. fee simple absolutes
   d. both a and b

19. Real property may include
   a. mineral rights
   b. airspace
   c. natural vegetation
   d. all of the above

20. Which of the following concepts is least associated with the others?
   a. estate for years
   b. periodic tenancy
   c. life estate

d. estate at will

21. Which of the following terms least belongs with the others?
    a. will
    b. implied warranty
    c. succession
    d. occupancy

22. Which of the following is (are) false?
    a. a testator devises personal property to legatees
    b. a will is also known as a testament
    c. both a and b
    d. neither a nor b

23. A legal procedure whereby a superior court in the county where the real property is located or where the deceased resided oversees the distribution of the decedent's property is called
    a. reliction
    b. testamentary dedication
    c. intestate succession
    d. probate

24. A nuncupative will is
    a. an oral will
    b. not valid in California
    c. both a and b
    d. neither a nor b

25. All wills must be witnessed by
    a. at least one competent witness
    b. at least two competent witnesses
    c. at least three competent witnesses
    d. none of the above

26. To acquire a prescriptive easement on a property, one need not
    a. use the property openly
    b. pay taxes on the property
    c. use the property adversely to the owner's interests
    d. both a and b

27. Alienation cannot be accomplished through
    a. gift
    b. public dedication

c. public grant
d. reliction

28. Which of the following terms least belongs with the others?
   a. will
   b. heir
   c. devisee
   d. testator

29. Delivery of a grant deed
   a. is necessary for a deed to be valid
   b. can be made within one year after the grantor's death
   c. satisfies all of the requirements to be able to record the deed
   d. both a and c

30. A grant deed would not be valid unless
   a. it is acknowledged
   b. it is signed
   c. it is recorded
   d. all of the above

31. The two general types of private ownership include
   a. joint ownership
   b. ownership in severalty
   c. ownership in reversion
   d. both a and b

32. Which of the following is (are) false?
   a. ownership in severalty refers to simultaneous ownership in several properties
   b. each of the partners of a general partnership is personally liable for all of the debts of the partnership
   c. both a and b
   d. neither a nor b

33. Which of the following is (are) false?
   a. community property is a form of joint ownership
   b. tenancy in partnership is a form of joint ownership
   c. both a and b
   d. neither a nor b

34. Unity of interest refers to

a. joint tenants must receive ownership in a property from the same deed
b. each of the joint tenants must acquire his/her interest in the property at the same time
c. each of the joint tenants must have an equal, undivided right to possession of the entire property
d. joint tenants having equal interests in a property

35. Bob and Jane own the property as joint tenants. Jane transfers her interest in the property to Bill and Susan, who are married. Which of the following is (are) false?
a. Bob is a joint tenant with Bill and Susan
b. Bill and Susan's interest in the property is community property
c. both a and b
d. neither a nor b

36. Jane and Bob acquire an undeveloped city lot as joint tenants. Jane marries Joe and conveys her interest in the joint tenancy to Joe without the knowledge or consent of Bob. Joe
a. is a joint tenant with Bob
b. is a tenant in common with Bob
c. has no interest in the lot because Jane could not transfer her interest without Bob's approval
d. none of the above

37. Which real estate owner usually has no personal liability in regard to property?
a. a joint tenant
b. a general partner
c. a limited partner
d. a tenant in common

38. The unities necessary to create a joint tenancy include
a. freehold estate
b. title
c. relationship
d. all of the above

39. Jane and Bob are joint tenants. Jane conveys one half of her interest to Susan. Ownership of the property is
    a. Jane, Bob, and Susan as joint tenants
    b. Jane and Susan as joint tenants; Bob as tenant in common
    c. Jane, Bob, and Susan as tenants in common
    d. Jane and Bob as joint tenants; Susan has no interest in the property

40. Jane and Susan own a condo as tenants in common. Susan dies having willed her interest to Joe.
    a. Jane owns the condo in severalty, free of Susan's debts
    b. Jane owns the condo in severalty, subject to Susan's debts
    c. Jane and Joe own the property as joint tenants
    d. none of the above

41. A lien can be
    a. voluntary
    b. involuntary
    c. either a or b
    d. neither a nor b

42. A court's final determination of the rights and duties of the parties in an action before it is called
    a. an abstract of judgment
    b. a judgment lien
    c. a fiduciary rendering
    d. a judgment

43. A judgment lien is
    a. an involuntary lien
    b. a general lien
    c. an official charge against property as security for the payment of a debt or an obligation owed for services rendered
    d. all of the above

44. Which of the following is (are) false?
    a. a judgment lien based on child support is good for 10 years and can be renewed
    b. liquidated damages is a sum of money that the parties agree will serve as the exact amount of damages that will be paid upon a breach of a contract

c. both a and b

d. neither a nor b

45. What is it that a judgment creditor must issue to the debtor upon the debtor's paying off a lien in full?
    a. liquidated lien certificate
    b. acknowledgment of satisfaction
    c. reconveyance deed
    d. none of the above

46. Janet was injured at a party in Joe's house. She obtained a $5,000 judgment against Joe and recorded an abstract of judgment. She has
    a. a specific lien
    b. a general lien
    c. a construction lien
    d. an attachment lien

47. Which of the following is a general lien?
    a. judgment lien
    b. mechanics lien
    c. property tax lien
    d. none of the above

48. An abstract of judgment is recorded
    a. before a writ of attachment
    b. after a judgment is entered
    c. before a lis pendens is filed
    d. both a and b

49. A recorded document that puts the public on notice that a certain property may be affected by the outcome of a lawsuit is
    a. lis pendens
    b. notice of pendency of action
    c. writ of execution
    d. both a and b

50. Which of the following has highest priority?
    a. a deed of trust recorded June 1, 2010

b. in mechanics lien recorded June 1, 2010

c. a property tax lien recorded June 1, 2011

d. a judgment lien recorded August 1, 2010

51. Which of the following is false?

a. in a listing agreement, a safety clause states that the property is in a condition safe to show to prospective buyers

b. an implied contract is implied by the actions or inactions of one or more of the parties

c. a principal is the one whom an agent represents

d. a court order that requires a person to perform according to the terms of a contract is an order for specific performance

52. Bob promises to pay Sally $20 if she mows his lawn by next Friday. Sally replies: "I'll see if I can." Sally mows Bob's lawn next Thursday.

a. Bob does not owe Sally $20 because she did not agree to the contract

b. Bob owes Sally $20

c. there was no contract because it was not in writing

d. none of the above

53. Which of the following terms least belongs with the others?

a. void

b. voidable

c. equitable title

d. legal effect

54. Which of the following is (are) false?

a. a void contract cannot be enforced by law

b. a contingency is an event that may happen, the occurrence upon which the happening of another event is dependent

c. both a and b

d. neither a nor b

55. Aliens

a. have the same rights to acquire and transfer property as citizens

b. are subject to certain property transfer reporting and tax withholding requirements

c. both a and b

d. neither a nor b

56. A contract that has been fully performed is an

a. executory contract

b.　executed contract

c.　unenforceable contract

d.　rescindable contract

57. Mutual consent is evidenced by
   a.　a lawful object

   b.　capable parties

   c.　offer and acceptance

   d.　a written document

58. The law that requires certain types of contracts be in writing in order for the contract to be enforceable is the
   a.　Statute of Executed Contracts

   b.　Statute of Limitations

   c.　Statute of Frauds

   d.　Statute of Enforceability

59. Which of the following is not an essential element of a valid contract?
   a.　writing

   b.　mutual consent

   c.　consideration

   d.　capable parties

60. After a certain time, a valid contract can become
   a.　voidable

   b.　unenforceable

   c.　illegal

   d.　void

61. A special relationship of trust and loyalty is known as
   a.　an actual agency

   b.　and ostensible agency

   c.　an agency by implication

   d.　a fiduciary relationship

62. When an agent is actually employed by the principal, the agency might be
   a.　an agency by ratification

b. an agency by express agreement

c. neither a nor b

d. either a or b

63. The fiduciary relationship that a real estate agent owes to his or her principal includes

a. the legal obligation of honesty

b. the legal obligation of disclosure

c. the legal obligation of utmost care

d. all of the above

64. Which of the following terms least belongs with the others?

a. estoppel

b. implication

c. ratification

d. express agreement

65. When an agency is created by an unauthorized agent who acts as if he or she is the agent of a principal, and this principal reasonably believes that the unauthorized agent is acting as his or her agent, the agency is created by

a. implication

b. estoppel

c. ratification

d. express agreement

66. Conversion is

a. an attempt by alchemists to convert silver into gold

b. the process of converting property into cash via a sales transaction

c. the failure to properly segregate the funds belonging to a broker from the funds received and held on behalf of the seller or buyer

d. none of the above

67. A broker may keep no more than how much of his or her personal funds in the broker's trust fund account?

a. $0

b. $100

c. $250

d. none of the above

68. A broker's trust fund records must be kept for a minimum of

a. 2 years

b. 3 years

c. 4 years

d. 5 years

69. A selling broker must deliver the agency disclosure form to the buyer before

a. the buyer signs the offer to buy

b. presenting the offer to the seller

c. the seller accepts the offer

d. none of the above

70. The maximum amount that a person can recover for a single transaction from the real estate Recovery Account is

a. $50,000

b. $100,000

c. $250,000

d. none of the above

71. George obtains a 30-year, 4½% level-payment loan of $500,000 to purchase a house. His monthly payments are $2,275. What is his interest charge for the second month?

a. $1,866.47

b. $1,873.50

c. $1,837

d. $1,875

72. Jennifer owns a rectangular lot that is 175 feet deep and 105 feet wide. She has contracted to have a 4 1/2 foot high fence built around the lot. Materials cost will be $.55 per square foot and the labor cost will be $2.15 per linear foot. What will the fence cost Jennifer?

a. $2,590.00

b. $46,682.12

c. $1,980.00

d. $1,295.00

73. A road runs along the west side of the S½ of the NW¼ of a section. If the road is 45 feet wide how many acres does the road contain?

a. 2.727 acres

b. .682 acres

c. 1.364 acres

d. .341 acres

74. A triangular lot with height 105 feet and width 95 feet sold for $12 per square foot. What did the lot sell for?

a. $119,700

b. $29,925

c. $55,775

d. $59,850

75. Julio sold a house for $475,000 and received $11,875 in commission. What commission rate did Julio receive on the sale?

a. 3%

b. 3.5%

c. 2%

d. none of the above

76. Of the following which, if any, is a purchase money loan?

a. a loan to fix the roof

b. a loan to remodel an owner-occupied house

c. neither a nor b

d. both a and b

77. Which of the following is (are) false?

a. one of the most important aspects of the Truth-in-Lending Act is to prevent charges and recording fees from exceeding a maximum of $700

b. one of the most important aspects of the Truth-in-Lending Act is to standardize the way in which certain costs of a loan are calculated and disclosed

c. both a and b

d. neither a nor b

78. Under a deed of trust, who holds equitable title to the property?

a. the trustee

b. the trustor

c. the beneficiary

d. the broker

79. A clause in a deed of trust that permits a later filed deed of trust to have greater priority is called

a. a subordination clause

b. a defeasance clause

160

c. an alienation clause

d. subrogation clause

80. A seller carry back loan is

   a. a purchase money loan where the mortgagee is a third-party lender that loans money (cash) that the borrower uses to acquire property

   b. a revolving line of credit provided by a home equity mortgage

   c. a security instrument for a loan for homeowners over the age of 62 who have a large amount of equity in their homes, usually designed to provide such homeowners with monthly payments, often over the lifetime of the last surviving homeowner who either moves out of the house or dies

   d. a loan or credit given by a seller of real property to a purchaser of that property

81. As a general rule, a true mortgage has how many parties?

   a. 1

   b. 2

   c. 3

   d. 4

82. Leverage refers to

   a. the ability of a lender to foreclose if the borrower defaults

   b. the maximum amount the interest rate can go up during the life of a loan

   c. a method of multiplying gains or losses on investments

   d. none of the above

83. A straight note provides for

   a. installments consisting of an equal amount of principal and interest

   b. installment payments that pay off the entire loan gradually over the life of the loan

   c. periodic payments that consist of interest only

   d. none of the above

84. A mortgage under which all periodic installment payments are equal is called

   a. an adjustable rate mortgage

   b. a level payment mortgage

c. a negative amortized loan

d. none of the above

85. The federal act that made due-on-sale provisions a federal issue is
   a. the Garn-St. Germain Act
   b. the Truth-in-Lending Act
   c. the Real Estate Settlement Procedures Act
   d. the Federal Alienation Act

86. Which of the following is (are) false?
   a. junior loans are made in the secondary market
   b. a conventional loan is a mortgage that is not FHA insured or VA guaranteed
   c. both a and b
   d. neither a nor b

87. Preapproval typically involves
   a. verification of income
   b. appraisal of the property securing the loan
   c. a guarantee that a loan will be approved
   d. both a and b

88. FHA stands for
   a. Federal Housing Association
   b. Federal Housing Assistance
   c. Federal Housing Agency
   d. none of the above

89. Which of the following terms least belongs with the others?
   a. source of income
   b. assets
   c. appraised value
   d. liabilities

90. Monthly car payments are likely to be included in
   a. front-end ratio
   b. back-end ratio
   c. PMI
   d. LTV

91. Which of the following terms least belongs with the others?

a. length of employment

b. investment income

c. back-end ratio

d. borrower's historical income

92. FHA loans
   a. can never exceed $417,500
   b. can never exceed $1 million
   c. can be for any amount
   d. none of the above

93. To obtain a VA loan, a veteran must obtain a
   a. certificate of eligibility
   b. certificate of appraisal
   c. certificate of MIP
   d. both a and b

94. The maximum amount of guarantee for a VA loan for a veteran with full eligibility is what percentage of the VA-determined county loan limit?
   a. 20%
   b. 25%
   c. 30%
   d. 35%

95. CalVet
   a. insures loans to veterans
   b. guarantees loans to veterans
   c. makes loans to veterans
   d. only purchases mortgages from approved lenders

96. Subjective value refers to
   a. market value
   b. the price actually paid for a property
   c. value due to any cause
   d. value placed on the amenities of a property by a specific person

97. The capitalization approach to value is also referred to as the

a. gross income approach
b. effective gross income approach
c. straight-line approach
d. income approach

98. The principle of progression states that
   a. real estate tends to increase in value over time
   b. property values are in a constant state of flux due to economic, environmental, political, social, and physical forces in the area
   c. the maximum value of property, its highest and best use, is created and maintained when land use by interacting elements of production are in equilibrium or balance
   d. the value of a residence of lesser value tends to be enhanced by proximity to residences of higher value

99. If a property has land value of $200,000, a structure with replacement cost of $375,000, and an estimated value of $500,000, what is the accrued depreciation of the structure?
   a. $125,000
   b. $75,000
   c. $325,000
   d. $50,000

100. The most probable price that a property should bring in a competitive market in which buyers and sellers are acting prudently is referred to as
   a. market value
   b. the value placed in a property by a specific person
   c. market price
   d. replacement cost

101. Subjective value is also known as
   a. market value
   b. residual value
   c. value in use
   d. none of the above

102. The capitalization approach to value is also referred to as the
   a. income approach
   b. cost approach
   c. straight-line method

d. none of the above

103. The principle of competition states that
    a. improvements made to a property will contribute to its value or that, conversely, the lack of a needed improvement will detract from the value of the property
    b. the best use of a property in terms of value is the use most likely to produce the greatest net return (in terms of money or other valued items, such as amenities) over a given period of time
    c. property values are in a constant state of flux due to economic, environmental, political, social, and physical forces in the area
    d. none of the above

104. The estimated value of a property is $500,000; land value is $200,000; and accrued depreciation of the structure is $75,000. What is the replacement cost of the structure?
    a. $300,000
    b. $225,000
    c. $325,000
    d. $375,000

105. The most probable price that a property should bring in a competitive market in which buyers and sellers are acting prudently is referred to as
    a. market price
    b. value placed on property by a specific person
    c. capitalization value
    d. market value

106. A neutral depository in which something of value is held by an impartial third party until all conditions specified in the escrow instructions have been fully performed is
    a. the administration of a loan from the time the loan proceeds are dispersed to the time the loan is paid off in full
    b. a report to be submitted on IRS Form 1099-S regarding the sale of real estate, giving the seller's name, Social Security number, and the gross sale proceeds

c. a settlement form mandated by RESPA for use in all purchases of owner-occupied residences of 1-4 dwelling units that use funds from institutional lenders regulated by the federal government
d. an escrow

107. An escrow agent should be someone with whom the
a. buyer can feel safe depositing the purchase price before receiving the deed
b. seller can feel safe depositing the deed before receiving the purchase price
c. both a and b
d. neither a nor b

108. A real estate broker who is not licensed as an escrow agent may always conduct an escrow
a. if the broker represents the seller
b. if the broker is a party to the transaction
c. neither a nor b
d. both a and b

109. An escrow agent is also referred to as an escrow
a. owner
b. holder
c. principal
d. beneficiary

110. The HUD-1 Uniform Settlement Statement is
a. mandated for use by RESPA in all commercial real estate transactions
b. only needs to be used for purchases of single-family homes if the loan does not come from a lender regulated by the federal government
c. is only used for seller carry back loans
d. none of the above

111. In case a controversy arises between the buyer and seller as to what certain escrow instructions mean, the escrow agent may
a. do what the seller wants
b. do what the buyer wants
c. do what the lender wants
d. none of the above

112. Which of the following terms least belongs with the others?

a. reserve account

b. title insurance

c. impound account

d. loan servicing

113. Accepting escrow instructions that contain one or more blanks to be filled in after the signing of the instructions and failing to deliver at the time of signing any instruction a copy thereof to all persons signing the instructions are

a. acts typically performed by escrow agents

b. acts typically performed by lenders

c. acts permitted by the CalBRE of real estate agents who act as escrow agents for real estate transactions that are they are involved in

d. none of the above

114. The California Withholding Law requires the withholding of what percent of the gross sales price in certain real estate transactions?

a. 2 1/3

b. 3 1/3

c. 3 2/3

d. 10

115. Loan servicing typically includes

a. sending monthly statements

b. collecting loan payments

c. both a and b

d. neither a nor b

116. Privity of estate is

a. a legal doctrine that states that a legally enforceable relationship exists between the parties who hold interests in the same real property

b. a legal doctrine that states that a legally enforceable relationship exists between the persons who are parties to a contract

c. both a and b

d. neither a nor b

117. Unless it is impractical to do so (such as in the case of an emergency), the landlord of a residential unit may enter the premises only if the landlord has an acceptable reason and
    a. the entry is made during normal business hours unless the tenant consents to the entry at the time of entry
    b. the landlord gives the tenant reasonable notice in writing of his or her intent to enter
    c. both a and b
    d. neither a nor b

118. A lease provides that the tenant pay a fixed rent plus some portion of the operating expenses of the premises might be a
    a. gross lease
    b. net lease
    c. triple net lease
    d. either b or c

119. An advantage of an unlawful detainer action is
    a. the tenant has only 10 days to respond
    b. the action is given priority over most other civil actions
    c. both a and b
    d. neither a nor b

120. If a tenant sublets his or her apartment, the tenant has
    a. transferred all of his or her interest in the leased premises
    b. transferred his or her rights to a portion of the premises
    c. transferred his or her rights to the entire premises for less than the entire remaining lease term
    d. either b or c

121. A legal doctrine that states that a relationship exists between parties who hold interests in the same real estate is
    a. novation
    b. privity of contract
    c. privity of chattel real
    d. none of the above

122. A landlord may enter a leased residential unit after giving proper notice
    a. to make necessary or agreed repairs

b. to ensure that the tenant is maintaining the premises in a neat condition

c. either a or b

d. neither a nor b

123. A lease that provides that the tenant will construct a building on the premises most likely is a

a. net lease

b. graduated lease

c. ground lease

d. percentage lease

124. A lease in a stripmall provides for rent payments based in part on a tenant's gross sales. The lease is a

a. graduated lease

b. net lease

c. ground lease

d. none of the above

125. A tenant who assigns his or her interest in a lease

a. transfers the tenant's right to less than all of the premises

b. transfers the entire premises for less than the entire remaining lease term

c. neither a nor b

d. either a or b

126. The California Factory Built Housing Law

a. provides local governments with the authority to convert blighted conditions within their jurisdictions

b. provides for the adoption of comprehensive, long-term general plans

c. refers to city and county ordinances that require builders to set aside a specific portion of new construction for people of low to moderate incomes

d. none of the above

127. A California law that is administered by the Real Estate Commissioner to protect purchasers from fraud, misrepresentation, or deceit in the initial sale of subdivided property is the

a. Subdivision Map Act
b. Interstate Land Sales Hold Disclosure Act
c. Rumford Act
d. Subdivided Lands Law

128. Pursuant to the Vacation Ownership and Time-Share Act of 2004, the purchaser of a time-share interest has how many days to cancel after receipt of the public report or after the date of signing the purchase agreement, whichever is later?
   a. 7
   b. 5
   c. 10
   d. 30

129. A planning commission makes recommendations to
   a. either a city council or county board of supervisors
   b. the CalBRE
   c. HUD
   d. California Attorney General

130. A common interest development is
   a. a subdivision in which owners own a partial or fractional interest in an entire parcel of land
   b. a subdivision in which purchasers own or lease a separate lot, unit, or interest, and have an undivided interest or membership in a portion of the common area of the subdivision
   c. a subdivision with no common areas of ownership or use among the owners of the subdivision parcels
   d. a subdivision not subject to a Mello-Roos lien

131. A property owner who can show damage to the value of his or her property that would far outweigh any benefits from enforcement of a zoning ordinance would apply for
   a. nonconforming use
   b. conditional use
   c. rezoning amendment
   d. none of the above

132. The Civil Rights Act of 1968 prohibits

a. steering

b. blockbusting

c. both a and b

d. neither a nor b

133. A zoning ordinance is likely to regulate

a. building heights

b. use of property

c. both a and b

d. neither a nor b

134. Several property owners believe that their area was improperly zoned. They should apply for

a. variance

b. nonconforming use

c. conditional use

d. none of the above

135. Of the following, which is an example of conditional use?

a. established property use that does not conform to new zoning requirements is permitted to continue

b. property owners who felt that their area was improperly zoned have successfully petitioned the zoning commission to amend the zoning ordinance

c. a property owner whose property would be unduly burdened has been permitted an exception to a zoning ordinance

d. none of the above

136. As an alternative to using 27½ years for the depreciable life of residential property and 39 years for nonresidential property, both types of property may use how many years as their depreciable lives?

a. 20

b. 25

c. 30

d. 40

137. "Book sale" is
   a. a phrase referring to the tax concept of depreciation
   b. a term referring to an accounting for tax purposes regarding delinquent property taxes
   c. cash and/or unlike property transferred in a 1031 exchange
   d. the sale of property on which book depreciation has been taken

138. The installment sales method can be used for
   a. the regular sales of inventory of personal property
   b. sales of stock or securities traded on established securities market
   c. both a and b
   d. neither a nor b

139. As a general rule government lands are
   a. taxed at a slightly lower rate than private property
   b. not taxed
   c. taxed at the same rate as private property
   d. allowed an exemption for half of the lands' fair market value

140. Cities in California
   a. may impose a documentary transfer tax higher than the county documentary transfer tax
   b. may not impose a documentary transfer tax; only counties can
   c. may impose a documentary transfer tax as long as it does not exceed the county documentary transfer tax
   d. may not impose a documentary transfer tax greater than 1% of the "full cash value"

141. As a general rule, for tax purposes the depreciable life of nonresidential properties is
   a. 27 years
   b. 27½ years
   c. 39½ years
   d. none of the above

142. If delinquent property taxes remain unpaid until the end of the fiscal year, the county tax collector publishes
   a. a writ of possession

b. an intent to sell

c. a cease-and-desist order

d. none of the above

143. An installment sale is a sale in which the seller

a. receives at least one payment in a later tax period

b. may report part of the gain from the sale for the year in which a payment is received

c. both a and b

d. neither a nor b

144. A buyer purchases a condo for $850,000, agreeing to pay $150,000 cash and to assume the seller's $700,000 outstanding loan on the house. Assuming that only the county (not the city) in which the property lies has a documentary transfer tax, how much would that tax be?

a. $165

b. $150

c. $935

d. $467.50

145. San Francisco has a documentary transfer tax

a. of $0.55 per $500 (or fraction thereof) of the transfer price

b. that varies depending on the sales price of the property

c. of $1.10 per $1,000 (or fraction thereof) of the transfer price

d. none of the above

146. A deficiency arising from poor architectural design is an example of

a. physical deterioration

b. external obsolescence

c. disintegration

d. functional obsolescence

147. A house with a stone exterior, rounded tower with a conical roof, and steeply pitched roof is likely to be a

a. French Normandy

b. French Provincial

c. Georgian Colonial

d. Dutch Colonial

148. EER (energy efficiency ratio) refers to
   a. a measure of heating capacity
   b. the measure of the resistance of insulation to heat transfer
   c. compression stresses
   d. none of the above

149. A sloping roof that rises from all four sides of a house is a
   a. gambrel roof
   b. hip roof
   c. gable roof
   d. shed roof

150. One board foot is
   a. 144 in.^{3} of lumber
   b. 24 in.^{3} of lumber
   c. 12 in.^{3} of lumber
   d. none of the above

Answers to Practice Exam #3

<u>Note</u>: If you would like to obtain a deeper understanding of the real estate principles behind the following answers, consult the textbook *California Real Estate Principles and License Preparation, 2nd Edition*, which is available both in print and Kindle formats on Amazon.com. The author, Jim Bainbridge, is a graduate of Harvard Law School, a member of the California Bar, and a licensed California real estate broker.

1. a. The treaty of Guadalupe Hidalgo was signed in 1848.

2. c. A bundle of rights may include the right to possess, use, enjoy, encumber, sell, and/or exclude from others.

3. c. The three broad categories of real property are land, appurtenances, and things affixed to the land.

4. a. Support rights, stock in a mutual water company, and easements appurtenant are appurtenant rights. Emblements are personal property.

5. d. Oil, gas, and geothermal steam are subject to the law of capture.

6. c. A commercial acre is the buildable part of an acre that remains after subtracting land needed for streets, sidewalks, and curbs. Because an acre equals 43,560 square feet, a commercial acre must contain less than 43,560 square feet.

7. d. Crops on leased land may be either personal or real property, depending on the lease terms.

8. d. Trade fixtures are objects that a tenant attaches to real property for use in the tenant's trade or business. Trade fixtures differ from other fixtures in that, even though they are attached with some permanence to real property, they may be removed at the end of the tenancy of the business if removal does not cause irreparable harm.

9. b. The law of capture is the legal right of a landowner to all of the gas, oil, and steam produced from wells drilled directly underneath on his or her property, even if the gas, oil, or steam migrates from below a neighbor's property.

10. a. A servient tenement is land that is burdened by an easement.

11. d. A mortgage, though an interest in real property, is not considered an estate.

12.   a. An estate for years has a definite fixed term; a periodic tenancy continues from period to period until terminated.

13.   d. The degree, quantity, nature, duration, and interest one has in real property is referred to as an estate.

14.   a. Zoning codes and building restrictions are examples of police power, but are not deed restrictions.

15.   b. When property is transferred, the law presumes that a fee simple absolute is being transferred.

16.   c. The term of a lease for agricultural land cannot exceed 51 years.

17.   d. The term of the lease for a city lot cannot exceed 99 years.

18.   b. A reversionary interest in a life estate is an interest in the property that reverts to the grantor at the termination of the life estate.

19.   d. In addition to land and buildings, real property may include mineral rights, airspace, and natural vegetation.

20.   c. An estate for years, a periodic tenancy, and an estate at will are less-than-freehold estates.

21.   b. Will, succession, and occupancy are ways of transferring or acquiring real property.

22.   a. A testator *bequeaths* personal property to legatees.

23.   d. A legal procedure whereby a superior court in the county where the real property is located or where the deceased resided oversees the distribution of the decedent's property is called probate.

24.   c. A nuncupative will is an oral will, which is no longer valid in California.

25.   d. Though all other types of wills must be witnessed to be valid, a holographic will need not be witnessed if the signature and the material provisions are in the handwriting of the testator.

26.   b. One need not pay taxes on the property in order to acquire a prescriptive easement on the property.

27.   d. Reliction is a natural process by which the owner of riparian or littoral property acquires additional land that has been covered by water but has become permanently uncovered by the gradual recession of water.

28.   b. An heir is a person entitled to obtain property through intestate succession.

29.   a. To be valid, a grant deed must be legally delivered.

30.   b. In order to be valid, a grant deed must be signed by the grantor.

31.   d. There are two general types of private ownership: ownership in severalty (the property is owned by one person only) and joint ownership or co-ownership (the property is owned by two or more persons).

32.   a. When one person is the sole owner of property, the property is owned in severalty.

33.   d. Both community property and tenancy in partnership are forms of joint ownership.

34.   d. Unity of interest refers to joint tenants having equal interests in a property.

35.   a. Bob would be a tenant in common with Bill and Susan, whose interest is community property, as it was acquired during marriage.

36.   b. Joe is a tenant in common with Bob. A joint tenant may transfer his or her interest without the consent of other joint tenants.

37.   c. A limited partner generally has no personal liability vis-à-vis his or her ownership of real property.

38.   b. The four unities of joint tenancy are possession, title, interest, and time.

39.   c. Because the transfer destroyed the unities of time and interest, Jane, Bob, and Susan are tenants in common.

40.   d. Jane and Joe would own the property as tenants in common.

41.   c. A lien can be either a voluntary lien (such as a deed of trust) or an involuntary lien, which is a lien created by operation of law, not by the voluntary acts of the debtor.

42.   d. A court's final determination of the rights and duties of the parties in an action before it is called a judgment.

43.   d. A judgment lien is an involuntary lien, a general lien, and an official charge against property as security for the payment of a debt or an obligation owed for services rendered.

44.   a. A judgment lien based on child support has no statutory limitation period.

45.   b. Once a judgment lien is paid off in full, the judgment creditor "shall immediately" issue an acknowledgment of satisfaction and file it with the court, thereby clearing the lien from the title to the property.

46.   b. The judgment was against Joe personally, so the abstract of judgment will attach to any property Joe has in any county in California in which the abstract of judgment is recorded.

47.   a. Mechanics liens and property tax liens are specific liens.

48.   b. An abstract of judgment is recorded after a judgment is entered.

49.   d. A notice of pendency of action, also known as a lis pendens, is a notice that provides constructive notice to potential purchasers or encumbrancers of a piece of real property of the pendency of a lawsuit in which an interest in that piece of real property is claimed.

50.   c. As a general rule, the order of payment is determined by the order of lien recording; in other words, first to record, first in priority. However, some types of liens are given special priority. Property tax liens and special assessment liens, for example, have priority over all other types of liens.

51.   a. A safety clause is a clause in a listing agreement that protects the broker's commission for a sale that is consummated after the termination of the broker's listing agreement to a buyer who is found by the broker during the term of the listing agreement.

52.   b. Bob and Sally had a unilateral contract. Sally performed, so Bob owes her $20.

53.   c. In regard to legal effect, a contract may be valid, void, voidable, or unenforceable.

54.   d. A void contract cannot be enforced by law. A contingency is an event that may happen, the occurrence upon which the happening of another event is dependent.

55.   c. Aliens have the same rights to acquire and transfer property as citizens; however, they are subject to certain transfer reporting and tax withholding requirements.

56.   b. An executed contract is a contract that has been fully performed. The term may also refer to a contract that has been signed by the parties to the contract.

57.   c. Mutual consent is evidenced by an offer and an acceptance.

58.   c. The statute of frauds is a law that requires certain types of contracts, including most real estate contracts, to be in writing and signed by the party to be bound in order for the contract to be enforceable.

59.   a. A valid contract does not have to be in writing.

60.   b. The statute of limitations requires particular types of lawsuits to be brought within a specified time after the occurrence of the event giving rise to the lawsuit.

61.   d. A special relationship of trust and loyalty is known as a fiduciary relationship.

62.   d. Actual agency can be created in three ways: by express agreement, by ratification, or by implication.

63.   d. A real estate broker owes to his principal a special relationship of trust and loyalty known as a fiduciary relationship, which imposes on real estate brokers many strict legal obligations of utmost care, honesty, disclosure, and fair dealing.

64.   a. Actual agency can be created in three ways: by express agreement, by ratification, or by implication. Ostensible agency is created by estoppel.

65.   a. Agency by implication is created by an unauthorized agent who acts as if he or she is the agent of a principal, and this principal reasonably believes that the unauthorized agent is acting as his or her actual agent.

66.   d. Conversion is the unauthorized misappropriation and use of another's funds or other property.

67.   d. A broker may keep no more than $200 of his or her personal funds in a trust fund account to pay service fees on the account.

68.   b. A broker's trust fund records must be kept for a minimum of 3 years.

69.   a. A selling broker must deliver the agency disclosure form to the buyer before the buyer signs the offer to buy.

70.   a. The maximum amount that a person can recover for a single transaction from the real estate Recovery Account is $50,000.

71.   b. George's per month interest rate is $4\frac{1}{2}\% \div 12 = .375\%$. Therefore, the interest payment during the first month is .375% of $500,000 = $1,875. Since he paid $2,275 for the first month, $400 went to paying down the principal. Therefore, for the second month, his interest charge would be .375% of $499,600 = $1,873.50.

72.   a. 175 ft. X 4.5 ft. = 1,575 ft.²
105 ft. x 4.5 ft. = 945 ft.²
Total = 2,520 ft.²
2,520 ft.² x $.55 = $1,386

175 ft. x 2 + 105 ft. x 2 = 560 linear feet
560 ft. x $2.15/ ft. = $1,204

$1,386 + $1,204 = $2,590

73.　　c. The road is $5,280 \div 4 = 1,320$ ft. long.
1,320 ft. x 45 ft. = 59,400 ft.²
59,400 ft.² ÷ 43,560 ft.²/acre = 1.364 acres.

74.　　d. ½ x 105 x 95 = 49,875 ft.²
49,875 ft.² x $12/ ft.² = $59,800

75.　　d. $11,875 ÷ $475,000 = 2.5%

76.　c. Neither a loan to remodel nor to repair a roof is a purchase money loan.

77.　　a. The Truth-in Lending Act does not prevent charges and recording fees from exceeding a maximum of $700.

78.　　b. Under a deed of trust, bare legal title is held by the trustee; equitable title is held by the trustor.

79.　　a. A subordination clause in a deed of trust permits a later filed the deed of trust to have greater priority.

80.　　d. A seller carry back loan is a loan or credit given by a seller of real property to purchaser of that property.

81.　　b. As a general rule, a true mortgage has two parties, the borrower and the lender.

82.　　c. Leverage refers to a method of multiplying gains or losses on investments, such as by using borrowed money to make the investments.

83.　　c. A straight note provides for periodic payments that consist of interest only.

84.　　b. A level payment mortgage is a mortgage under which all periodic installment payments are equal.

85.　　a. The Garn-St. Germain Act is a federal law that made enforceability of due-on-sale provisions a federal issue.

86.　c. Junior loans are made in the primary mortgage market.

87.　　a. A preapproval typically involves verifying the potential borrower's income and credit but not an appraisal of the property.

88.　　d. FHA is an acronym for Federal Housing Administration.

89.　　c. Source of income, assets, and liabilities are the main determinants of a borrower's capacity to pay.

90. b. Back-end ratio is the ratio of total monthly expenses, including housing expenses and long-term monthly debt payments (including such items as car payments), to monthly gross income.

91. c. Length of employment, investment income, and a borrower's historical income are components of the potential borrower's capacity to repay the loan.

92. c. FHA loans can be for any amount, but the FHA insures loans only up to a maximum amount that varies from area to area.

93. a. To obtain a VA loan, a veteran must obtain a certificate of eligibility for himself or herself and a certificate of reasonable value on the property.

94. b. The maximum amount of guarantee for a veteran with full entitlement is 25% of the VA-determined county loan limit.

95. c. CalVet makes loans directly to veterans.

96. d. Subjective value and value in use refer to value placed on the amenities of a property by a specific person.

97. d. The capitalization approach is also referred to as the income approach.

98. d. The principle of progression states that the value of a residence of lesser value tends to be enhanced by proximity to residences of higher value.

99. b. Property value = land value + replacement cost - accrued depreciation. Therefore,
accrued depreciation = land value + replacement cost - property value
= $200,000 + $375,000 - $500,000 = $75,000.

100. a. Market value is the most probable price that a property should bring in a competitive and open market under all conditions requisite to a fair sale, the buyer and seller, each acting prudently, knowledgeably and assuming the price is not affected by undue stimulus.

101. c. Subjective value is also referred to as value in use.

102. a. The income approach to value is also referred to as the capitalization approach.

103. d. The principle of competition states that increased competition results in increased supply in relation to demand, and thereby to lower profit margins.

104. d. Replacement cost = $500,000 - $200,000+ $75,000 = $375,000.

105. d. Market value is most probable price which a property should bring in a competitive and open market under all conditions requisite to a fair sale, the buyer and seller each acting prudently, knowledgeably and assuming the price is not affected by undue stimulus.

106. d. An escrow is a neutral depository in which something of value is held by an impartial third party (called the escrow agent) until all conditions specified in the escrow instructions have been fully performed.

107. c. An escrow agent is someone with whom buyer can feel safe depositing the purchase price before receiving the deed, the seller can feel safe depositing the deed before receiving the purchase price, and the lender can feel secure that none of its loan funds will be disbursed until the promissory note and the deed of trust (or mortgage) are signed by the buyer.

108. a. A broker may conduct an escrow if the broker represents the seller or buyer, or the broker is a party to the transaction *and* performs an act for which a real estate license is required.

109. b. An escrow agent is also referred to as an escrow holder.

110. d. RESPA requires the use of the HUD-1 Uniform Settlement Statement for all purchases of owner-occupied residences of 1-4 dwelling units that use funds from institutional lenders regulated by the federal government.

111. d. In case a controversy arises between the buyer and seller as to what certain escrow instructions mean, the escrow agent may petition a court through interpleader to decide the issue.

112. b. Loan servicing often entails the establishment of a reserve account, which is also referred to as an impound account.

113. d. Accepting escrow instructions that contain one or more blanks to be filled in after the signing of the instructions, and failing to deliver at the time of signing any instruction a copy thereof to all persons signing the instructions are acts that are prohibited by the CalBRE.

114. b. Though there are exceptions, as a general rule the California Withholding Law requires the withholding of 3 1/3% of the gross sales price; therefore answer b is the best answer here.

115. c. Loan servicing typically includes sending monthly statements, collecting loan payments, and maintaining records of payments and balances due.

116. a. Privity of estate is a legal doctrine that states that a legally enforceable relationship exists between the parties who hold interests in the same real property.

117. c. Unless it is impractical to do so (such as in the case of an emergency), the landlord of a residential unit may enter the premises only if the landlord has an acceptable reason, the entry is made during normal business hours unless the tenant consents to the entry at the time of entry, and the landlord gives the tenant reasonable notice in writing of his or her intent to enter.

118. d. Under both a net lease and a triple net lease the tenant pays some portion of the operating expenses. In a triple net lease that "some portion" is usually 100%.

119. b. A tenant has only 5 days in which to respond to an unlawful detainer complaint.

120. d. A sublease is a transfer of a tenant's right to a portion of the leased premises or to the entire premises for less than the entire remaining lease term.

121. d. Privity of estate is a legal doctrine that states that a legally enforceable relationship exists between the parties who hold interests in the same real property.

122. a. Ensuring that the premises are being kept neat is not one of the acceptable reasons for landlord entry, regardless of notice.

123. c. A ground lease is a lease under which a tenant leases land and agrees to construct a building or to make other significant improvements on the land.

124. d. The lease is a percentage lease.

125. c. An assignment of a lease transfers the tenant's entire interest in the leased premises for the duration of the lease term.

126. d. The California Factory Built Housing Law regulates factory built housing.

127. d. The Subdivided Land Law is a California law that is administered by the Real Estate Commissioner to protect purchasers from fraud, misrepresentation, or deceit in the initial sale of subdivided property.

128. a. This Act specifically requires that in space immediately above the signature of the purchaser of a time-share interest a notice of cancellation be printed, stating that the purchaser has 7 days to cancel after receipt of the public report or after the date of signing the purchase agreement, whichever is later.

129. a. The general plan for each city and county is proposed by a planning commission (also referred to as a planning agency), whose members are appointed by the city council or county board of supervisors. The

planning commission makes recommendations to the relevant legislative body (city council or board of supervisors), which renders the final decision on the plan.

130. b. A common interest development is a subdivision in which purchasers own or lease a separate lot, unit, or interest, and have an undivided interest or membership in a portion of the common area of the subdivision.

131. d. A property owner who can show damage to the value of his or her property that would far outweigh any benefit from enforcement of a zoning ordinance would apply for a variance.

132. c. The Civil Rights Act of 1968 prohibits both steering and blockbusting.

133. c. Zoning ordinances of a city or county specify the type of land-use that is acceptable in certain areas, including heights of buildings.

134. d. A rezoning amendment is an amendment to a zoning ordinance that property owners may request if they feel that their area has been improperly zoned.

135. d. Conditional use is a zoning exception for special uses such as churches, schools, and hospitals that wish to locate to areas zoned exclusively for residential use.

136. d. As an alternative to using 27½ years for the depreciable life of residential property and 39 years for nonresidential property, both types of property may use 40 years as their depreciable lives.

137. b. "Book sale" is a term referring to an accounting for tax purposes regarding delinquent property taxes.

138. d. The installment sales method cannot be used for the regular sale of inventory of personal property, sales of stock or securities traded on established securities markets, or dealer sales (sales of real property held for sale to customers in the ordinary course of a trade or business, or regular sales of the same type of personal property) even if the sale is made in installments..

139. b. As a general rule, government lands are exempt from property taxation.

140. a. Cities may also impose a documentary transfer tax, which vary among the cities and can be much higher than the county transfer tax.

141. d. As a general rule, for tax purposes the depreciable life of nonresidential properties is 39 years.

142. b. If delinquent real property taxes remain unpaid until June 30, the county tax collector publishes an "intent to sell" the property.

143. c. An installment sale is a sale in which the seller receives at least one payment in a later tax period and may report part of the gain from the sale (as well as any interest received) for the year in which a payment is received.

144. a. The documentary transfer tax is only applied to the cash paid and, therefore, in this case is $1.10 x 150 = $165.

145. b. San Francisco, being both a county and the city, has a combined county/city documentary transfer tax that varies from $5.00 per $1,000 to $25.00 per $1,000, depending on the sales price of the property.

146. d. Functional obsolescence results (1) from deficiencies arising from poor architectural designs, out-dated style or equipment, and changes in utility demand, such as for larger houses with more garage space, and (2) from over-improvements, where the cost of the improvements was more than the addition to market value.

147. a. A French Normandy typically has stone a exterior with asymmetrical plan, a round tower with conical roof, and a steeply pitched roof.

148. d. Energy efficiency ratio (EER) refers to the ratio of the cooling capacity to power consumption of a room air conditioner.

149. b. A hip roof is a sloping roof that rises from all four sides of the house.

150. a. One board foot is 144 in.^{3} of lumber.